D0917612

# Waiting on the Sky

## More Flyover People Essays

Also by Cheryl Unruh

*Flyover People: Life on the Ground in a Rectangular State*

# Waiting on the Sky

## More Flyover People Essays

Cheryl Unruh

2014

Waiting on the Sky: More Flyover People Essays

Copyright © 2014 by Cheryl Unruh.

Quincy Press
Box 1215
Emporia, KS 66801
www.quincypress.com

Used with permission: Lisa Moritz' lyrics in "Here We Know" from her CD, *Dream of Blue*.

All photographs on the cover of and inside *Waiting on the Sky* are by Dave Leiker.

Book design and editing by Leon Unruh.

ISBN 978-0-692-20495-5

Library of Congress Control Number: 2014907459

Printed by Mennonite Press, Inc., in Newton, Kansas, USA.

*For my mother, Anita Byers,*
*who has taught me more than I'll ever know.*

# CONTENTS

## The Elements

## Departures

## Being a Kid

## Navigating Our Lives

# INTRODUCTION

Two-thirds of our view in Kansas is of the sky. In many areas of the state, we can stand on flat ground, spin in a circle and see 360 degrees of horizon.

The sky is always a big story on the Great Plains. We rely on the sky for our agricultural economy, for our health and well-being. It's also our entertainment. We watch storm clouds build and threaten us on spring evenings. We follow lazy clouds across the sky on summer afternoons. We chase sunsets.

Under that ever-changing sky we live our days on the wind-blown ground, on 82,000 square miles of earth. Kansas has 105 counties and 626 incorporated cities; 480 of those towns have fewer than 1,500 people. This is a rural state.

Born in central Kansas, I grew up on this land. I watched my dad and brother dig graves for our neighbors. During my high school years, my friends and I carried machetes into fields and we cut out the tall stalks of milo. I spent evenings watching the sun set from atop Pawnee Rock State Park, a famous lookout along the Santa Fe Trail. As a little kid, I rode with my dad on his school bus route. My mom taught me how to drive on the country roads. The grid of landscape is burned into my consciousness.

I love this land. I love this sky. I want you to love it also.

*Our Kansas*

*January 2011*

# AD ASTRA

John J. Ingalls gave us the best motto a state could ask for: Ad astra per aspera.

And if you're not into Latin: To the stars through difficulties.

Yeah, yeah, difficulties, we've had them before and we are up to our budgets in difficulties now, but I really like that "to the stars" part of the motto.

Ad astra stretches our thoughts, even our eyes, sends them both into the atmosphere. And that big old sky of ours, bursting with blue in the daytime, full of glittering stars at night, gives us endless space on which to scatter our dreams.

That's the good part, ad astra.

The other part of the phrase is per aspera. This is the line that builds character, makes us work hard, keeps us humble.

Our motto writer, Ingalls, lived through some of those difficult pre-state years. He arrived in the Kansas Territory in 1859, worked as a lawyer in Atchison and was a member of the Wyandotte Constitutional Convention. Ingalls became a state senator in 1862 and later served Kansas as a U.S. senator for 18 years. A likeness of Ingalls stands in National Statuary Hall in Washington, D.C.

As the motto suggests, it was a tough road getting Kansas admitted to the Union. And there have been many per aspera years since, including, but not limited to: 1863, Quantrill's raid on Lawrence; 1874, grasshopper plague; 1918, influenza pandemic; 1935, dust storms; 1951, flood; 1966, Topeka tornado; 2007, Greensburg tornado.

Our sesquicentennial year, 2011, meant to be a year of celebration, will be a year of additional devastating budget cuts. So we can expect a few discouraging words to be heard this year.

Perhaps it's our open and unburdened topography that saves us from utter despair when crises hit. Our close connection to the land keeps us grounded. And with two-thirds of our view as sky, we can't help but look up, gaze into to the blue background, the passing clouds, and at night, the stars.

Clyde Tombaugh looked up. He moved to Burdett with his family when he was 16. He ground his own lenses and mirrors and built a telescope in his quest to study the stars and planets. After drawing detailed sketches of Jupiter and Mars, he contacted Lowell Observatory in Arizona. They were impressed with Tombaugh and offered him a job. And the rest is history. (Including Pluto.)

Tombaugh discovered Pluto in 1930. And, for decades, we celebrated that planet as one of our own. Unfortunately, Pluto was downsized to a dwarf planet in 2006 by the International Astronomical Union.

During her childhood years in Atchison, Amelia Earhart surely spent time looking at the sky and dreaming. And in 1937, she and navigator Fred Noonan set out to circle the globe in a Lockheed Electra and never came down to earth, as far as we know. Current DNA testing of bones found on a deserted South Pacific island may prove otherwise.

Many other residents have sent their energies upward including Wichitans Walter and Olive Ann Beech, Clyde Cessna, Bill Lear, and others who have tested their locally built planes in the airspace over Kansas.

To help keep our vision aimed toward the heavens, the Cosmosphere in Hutchinson tells the story of space exploration.

And our "to the stars" motto became art. A Kansa warrior, "Ad Astra," created in bronze by Salina artist Richard Bergen, now stands atop the Kansas Capitol.

The Kansa warrior holds a powerful stance on the copper dome, bow in full draw, his arrow pointed toward the North Star.

At times, the state of the world and the state of the state can seem uncertain, but the celestial bodies remain steady. And in case we need reassurance, "Ad Astra" stands ready to show us the way to the stars.

*December 2010*

# 2011 — THE YEAR OF KANSAS

One hundred and fifty years. Yes, this year we celebrate the glory of Kansas.

Perhaps a short review is in order. A good place to start is the inland sea that once covered our state millions of years ago. That sea gave us our stash of limestone — and some incredible fossils.

Before they were so rudely interrupted, among others, the Kiowa, Kansa and Osage called this place home. By way of the Louisiana Purchase in 1803, the region became part of the United States.

As you well know, statehood did not come easy for Kansas. Before the 34th star was sewn onto the American flag, the Kansas Territory saw the Pottawatomie and Marais des Cygne Massacres and the Battle of Black Jack.

The Atchison, Topeka and Santa Fe Railroad laid tracks across the state. Kansas Pacific and Katy locomotives have chugged over our prairies. We also had the Underground Railroad, but it barely made a sound.

Kansas has 105 counties, four seasons, and one Cowtown. Here you'll find plains and prairies, Red Hills, Flint Hills and Smoky Hills. We even have glacier-carved hills, so for a flat state we do pretty well in the hill department.

Kansas has been home to aviators, astronauts, exodusters, cowboys. The Chisholm Trail, Oregon Trail and the Pony Express all galloped through Kansas. From 1854 to 1861, the Kansas Territory stretched to the eastern range of the Rocky Mountains. We owned Denver and Pike's Peak until someone redrew the map.

Outsiders may be puzzled by our mascots, but we cheer for the Jayhawks, the Shockers, and the Ichabods. Ichabod Washburn, who gave money and his name to Topeka's university, was an industrialist, not a fictional character.

But I'm sure the mention of Ichabod put them in your head, so let's talk cranes. We get excited when the endangered whooping cranes make their autumn layover at Cheyenne Bottoms.

Kansas has a rainbow of rivers: the Blue, the Verdigris, the Black Vermillion. This region was once called The Great American Desert. April 14, 1935, was dubbed Black Sunday because of a smothering dust storm. The 1951 flood brought a different kind of misery.

The Bloody Benders wielded a hammer, killing unsuspecting travelers. Carry Nation aimed to cut out alcohol with her hatchet. Quantrill destroyed lives with guns and fire. Dr. Samuel Crumbine fought the spread of disease with his slogan, "Don't spit on the sidewalk," which was printed on bricks.

Susanna M. Salter didn't run for office, but in Argonia in 1887, she was the first elected woman mayor in the United States. In 1912, Kansas women obtained the right to vote, eight years before the 19th Amendment was ratified.

Charles Curtis spoke French and Kansa before he learned English. In 1928, Curtis became the first U.S. vice president with Native American ancestry. Dwight Eisenhower named the presidential hideaway Camp David, after his grandson.

In 1887, salt was discovered in Reno County. Helium was found under Dexter in 1903. Drilling in the Stapleton Field in 1915 started Butler County's oil boom.

History books tell about the Kansas this used to be and the Kansans who have come before us. That covers the first 150 years. Now it's our turn to leave a mark and make this place even better. Long live the great state of Kansas.

*January 2014*

# NAMING NAMES

Once upon a time in Kansas, there were towns called Milo, Mimosa and Moonlight.

Those towns have faded into history now, but they are three of the 4,281 post offices established in Kansas between 1828 and 1961.

In a book called *Kansas Post Offices*, Robert W. Baughman listed every office opened (and closed) during those years. Baughman writes that 1879 was the year with the highest number of post offices established: 254. The year with the most discontinued offices was 1887 when 225 offices closed.

It is simply a book of lists. It has an alphabetical chart of every post office, a list by county, and a territorial list of post offices before statehood.

These towns came to life, many of them briefly, and most have now been returned to dust.

This week, Kansas claims 153 years of statehood. And to celebrate, I've been reading the names of towns in this book. I just love the sound of them. Kalvesta, Kanopolis, Kalamazoo.

We've had a Topsy, Tonovay, Tonganoxie, Thrall and even a Taos.

Cairo, Jerusalem, Jericho.

Vera, Verdi, Vassar. Hope and Hopewell.

Peacock, Bird City, Bird Nest, Birdton. And near Cheyenne Bottoms is a place called Redwing.

Skidmore and Skiddy. Prosper and Progress. And once upon a time, people picked up mail in Cowboy and in Plowboy.

Peru still stands in Chautauqua County. In Republic County, New Scandinavia is now Scandia.

Novelty once existed. As did Nonchalanta and Neutral.

Plano and Plato. And Radical City.

We've had a Quarry and Quincy, Quenemo, Quindaro and Quivera. There's been a Zephyr and Zenith, Zoro, Zulu and Zyba.

I would like to have visited Mystic, but this Sheridan County post office was only open from 1887 to 1889.

What's the story, I wonder, behind the town named Troublesome? And the one called Discord?

Kansas has had places called Neighborville, Paradise and Mt. Pleasant. We've had Love Joy, Valentine and Harmony. And Friendship, Good Intent and Free Will.

There was a Netherland once. Norway and Egypt. Denmark. Golden Belt, Golden Gate, Golden City. Globe.

I've been to Susank and Schoenchen, Speed and Spearville, but not to Scipio or Spivey.

Grasshopper Falls was renamed Sautrell Falls, which later became Valley Falls.

Delano is now a neighborhood in Wichita. We've had Dillwyn in Stafford County, Delavan in Morris. There was once a Dixie, a Cleveland, Key West and Brooklyn. And a California.

Comet and Coyote are long gone. In Marion County, Antelope once had a post office; Bison remains in Rush County. In Butler County, a town called Cloud became Andover.

Riley County, naturally, once had a place named Wild Cat, while Jay Hawk made an appearance in Chautauqua County.

Kansans have lived in Assaria, Argyle and Appomattox. Arcola, Aroma, Achilles. Long ago, residents picked up mail in Alfalfa and Wheatland and Cactus.

Over the years, we've used up a lot of post offices and towns in this state. The hardiest ones have survived. No matter which post office delivers your mail today, I send you joyous Kansas Day greetings.

*January 2010*

# SOUNDS LIKE KANSAS

As we make our homes here on the range, we'll stop to enjoy the honking of geese overhead.

We cheer at the brassiness of the school fight song and listen to a herd of basketball shoes pounding their way down the court.

While we're all pretty good at describing the Kansas we see and know — the landscape, weather, the politics, the people — how often do we pay attention to the sounds that Kansas offers?

Hearing seems secondary to sight, but sound is story — it is conversations, rhythms and melodies, it is movement, it is life itself.

Sound is the applause of cottonwood leaves in the breeze, it's the trash truck slamming one down on Monday mornings, the ding-ding-ding as the red and white bars block the railroad crossing.

During the day, the rumble of a freight train blends into the background, but at night, we hear the train charge into town and listen to the rhythm of the rails, the whistle cutting through the clean black air.

Deep in snow, the city moves in a hush as traffic sounds are absorbed by the powder. Then you hear the scrape of shovel against sidewalk.

In some communities the fire whistle blows every day at noon, and converts itself into a tornado siren as the need arises. The siren sends a circle of screams, telling us the skies have turned violent, that trouble is on its way.

Thunder is a sound Kansans will be hearing again soon. Purple storms will march in from the west with all the splash and hoopla they can manage, including a couple of elephants rolling across the sky.

So on a night in March you might be sleeping, your face soft against the pillow when an airplane-crash of lightning lands outside your bedroom window. The panes rattle, the house quivers, your eyes fly open and your feet hit the floor just out of instinct.

Wind is a constant in our lives. That breeze may be a nuisance, but it also makes music as it blows through the tall grasses in the Flint Hills.

Farm sounds are familiar to many — cattle lowing in the corral and chickens clucking. There's the squeaking of hinges on the old washhouse door, and the twitter of a meadowlark sitting on a barbed-wire fence.

You might drive past a school during recess and hear the shouts of kids as they chase one another in a game of tag. Their shouting might stir us to remember our own recesses, the school bell that called us in, those mornings when we each put hand to heart, "I pledge allegiance to the flag . . ."

Our childhoods were full of sound — the snapping of playing cards on bicycle spokes, a splash into the swimming pool, wet feet running on concrete, the lifeguard's whistle.

And we might remember lying in a patch of cool clover in our own front yard, listening as a single-engine airplane tried out the big blue sky above us. Other days we likely jumped when we heard an unexpected sonic boom, a jet breaking the sound barrier.

Maybe we tune in to sound only when the dog barks at the edge of the yardlight's circle, or when the coyotes have a hill-to-hill conversation, or when a guitar, banjo, and fiddle start weaving their tunes on a brick street on a Friday night.

Kansas is a beautiful state to look upon with its endless land and spacious sky. But some of its beauty is beyond vision — and to see the whole picture, it may help to close our eyes.

*January 2009*

# POSITIVES AND NEGATIVES

Some outsiders fail to recognize the beauty of Kansas.

There's nothing there," they scoff. "It's treeless, it's empty, it's flat."

As if those are bad things.

On Thursday, we celebrate the 148th anniversary of statehood. And I suppose it's fair to examine the so-called negative aspects of Kansas as well as the positive ones.

Others may blast our open topography, but I say Kansas has atmosphere. And plenty of it. We have 180 degrees of atmosphere — from horizon to horizon — thanks to that flat land of ours.

Montana, part of which is heavy with mountains, slings the slogan "Big Sky Country." But if you look above the Kansas prairie, I think you'll find we have just as much, if not more, sky here.

While the Rocky Mountains have the most breathtaking scenery I've encountered, the vertical landscape can seem claustrophobic; it's like living between parentheses.

In the Colorado Rockies, unless you're at the top of a mountain, you are offered only a fragment of sky. Direct sunlight is limited, available from about 10 a.m. to 3 p.m.

In Kansas we may not have purple mountain majesties, but we lay claim to the spacious skies and amber waves of grain. There are no mountains here to cut into our daylight hours or clip away at our blue sky. We are giddy with airspace.

While other states are cluttered with forests or mountains or major metropolitan areas, we are blessed with a Zen-like landscape, the prairie.

Singer-songwriter Lisa Moritz grew up in Tipton and now

lives in Emporia. Her song "Here We Know" describes so well what we appreciate in Kansas.

Lisa wrote, "Here a constant quiet beauty rises from a tall grass floor. Low hills move, a body breathing, under sky where less is more.

"Here we know the solid comfort that comes from living near the earth. Nothing here to scrape the sky but blade of windmill, wing of bird."

Yes, less is more. We value our negative space.

In art, negative space is that part of a photograph or a painting that is not the center of attention. Negative space is silence, background, an empty place where your eyes can rest. You may feel peaceful while gazing toward a grassy pasture, or you can rest your eyes upon the sky, that calming blue presence with its free-range clouds.

Here, we have the Flint Hills, a restful place for the soul, an open sanctuary in which the sky is our prayer book, the wind our hymnal.

After dark, we step into a cave of stars. In the big ol' night sky, we draw our own constellations. We connect the dots, creating a Native American warrior or maybe a fearsome John Brown.

With our heads leaned back, we can count white lights till we're dizzy. Out on the grassland we can almost hear the twinkling of those stars.

When Ian Frazier visited Kansas while writing his book *Great Plains*, he found that the topography contributes to our well-being.

Frazier happened to be in Nicodemus, an African-American community in western Kansas, during the town's annual gathering of descendants. In the township hall, a crowd watched six sisters dance. He said, "Suddenly I felt a joy so strong it almost knocked me down."

"Joy seems to be a product of the geography, just as deserts can produce mystical ecstasy and English moors produce gloom. Once happiness gets rolling in this open place, not much stops it," Frazier wrote.

We have a good thing going here in Kansas — the sky is big, the negatives are positive, and happiness just keeps rolling along.

*November 2013*

# AT HOME IN THE FLINT HILLS

Most of us have a favorite place on the planet, a place where we feel most like our real selves.

Maybe your favorite spot is in the Rocky Mountains, or on a tropical beach, or at your grandparents' farmhouse. Every time you arrive, it wraps its arms around you and says, "Welcome home, Sweetie."

We all understand the power that a particular spot can hold. For many of us, a favorite place is the Flint Hills.

These Flint Hills are not my native landscape. I was raised in central Kansas in the Arkansas River Valley. It's flat out there, mostly cropland. The agricultural grid pretty much guarantees a crossroad every mile. Barton County is more arid than here and short buffalo grass grows in the pastures, not tallgrass.

I love the Flint Hills now, but honestly, it took me a number of years to fully appreciate them. I was 21 when I moved to Emporia, and at that time my attention and youthfulness were focused on other things.

Back then, I stayed on paved roads. And while the turnpike provides a stunning trip through the heart of the Flint Hills, that decade wasn't a time in my life when I was entertained by topography.

At some point, I began to explore. In my late 20s, I made my first trek onto the open range in Chase County. My friend's pickup bounced over the cattle guard; this was the entry point onto a foreign landscape.

At one spot, the road crossed a rocky creek bed. "Really?" I asked. "We drive through a stream?" I had never forded a stream before. My previous life had shown me only bridges.

This summer I hiked trails at the Tallgrass Prairie National

Preserve just north of Strong City. The Fox Creek Trail winds along a shaded stream, but the trails in the hills are the ones that offer views of infinity.

In the Flint Hills, I feel a happy sense of solitude even in the company of others. And when I'm by myself, I never feel alone.

It's quiet on the prairie, but not always silent. Insects and birds chatter. Some days there's a growl of wind as gusts sweep the prairie without regard for man or beast. Wind can spin like a dervish, or it can ride low and slow and straight over the grasses, playing them like flutes.

A herd of bison lives on the preserve. Bulky and brown, they stand still like paperweights, holding down the prairie on those windy days.

The treeless landscape is one hill folding into another, bodies of hills lying together. We make our own shadows here, unless a cloud runs interference with the sun.

As a hawk glides overhead, we feel the rhythms of land and sky. Here, we step into that space between questions and answers, a place where we are satisfied with the unknown.

After dark, the wind settles down, and the Milky Way flings itself across the sky. A rumor of coyotes hangs in the night air.

When the world closes up shop, when the sky turns from blue to black for the very last time, when the final poem is written and read, this is where I want to be — out in my beloved Flint Hills.

*July 2013*

# 'DUST IN THE WIND'

Over the past few weeks, I've taken drives into the country looking for combines. And I've found them chugging through fields of gold, their shapes nearly obscured by self-created clouds of dust.

The combines eat their fill, separate wheat from chaff, then discharge the grain into waiting trucks. Harvest is man and machine, a season of agricultural glory.

This is a huge Kansas event, and harvest has its own culture. Although we get to eat the fruits of labor of these Kansas farmers, most of us who live in the city miss out entirely on the harvest experience.

My grandparents were farmers. As a 4-year-old, I was handed up the rungs of a combine's metal ladder where I joined my grandfather on his open-to-the-sky driver's seat. Wearing a straw hat for shade, Grandpa wrapped his left arm around me, his right hand grabbed the steering wheel, and we took a couple of spins through the field on that red dinosaur.

We shouldn't underestimate the power that childhood moments have on us as adults. Those feel-good times are things that we long to experience again.

Grandpa died when I was in first grade. Uncle Laramie took over the planting, but the harvest was outsourced to the Hawkins family, a custom-cutting crew from Oklahoma who followed the North Star every summer.

Each year when the Hawkins crew returned, my dad took my brother and me out to Grandma's farm to check on the harvest. At dusk, Dad visited with the cutters, pleasant men with faded shirts and sun-worn faces. In the creases of their necks were lines of paste, a mixture of dust and sweat.

After Grandpa died, I was a step removed from the harvest. My brother and cousins and I no longer helped Grandma pack her fried chicken to take to the fields like we did when Grandpa and my uncles ran the show.

But in the '60s and '70s, harvest brought life to our sleepy town of Pawnee Rock. The streets, normally as empty as a yawn, were suddenly busy with grain trucks which parked along Pawnee Avenue, in line to be weighed at the Farmers Elevator.

Willard Wilson, a welder who had a shop in town, was always in demand during harvest. Willard kept long hours in June and July, mending metal.

My friends and I idled on the lumberyard bench and waved at "the wheaties" when they drove past. Marilyn and Sarah were lucky enough to live across the street from the elevator. We should've opened a lemonade stand in their front yard.

Occasionally, on a dare, my friends and I sidled up to a truck and spoke with one of the teen drivers. He likely told us that he was from a faraway state such as Texas or South Dakota, an exotic place that we could only imagine.

One year, in the late '80s, my dad made arrangements for me to ride on a combine. I think the driver was probably part of the Hawkins team. A cloud of dust settled when he stopped the machine, waiting for me to cross the stubble in the half-cut field.

This combine even had a stereo system in its air-conditioned cab. As the header gnawed through the wheat, a familiar Kansas song played on the combine's radio: "Dust in the Wind."

And that has been my harvest song ever since. Whenever I hear that tune, I see myself climbing aboard that red combine to sit in the shade of my Grandpa and his old straw hat.

*November 2010*

# SUNSET ALERT

Some of the best sunsets happen in my rearview mirror.

That was the case one October evening. I was eastbound, driving from Garden City to Dodge City, when a gorgeous sunset sneaked up behind me.

The sky struck its best pose of the day. Golden end-of-time rays streamed from purple and crimson clouds. As I caught the sky-shattering color in my mirror, I noticed a lone elevator in the foreground, which would've been perfect to help frame a photograph.

Unfortunately, it was not until a mile or so later that I was able to pull off of the highway and into a rest area. As I jumped out of my car, another woman leapt from her Maryland-tagged vehicle, camera in hand. Together we snapped photos of the sunset, but the energy of the colors had drained. We were two minutes too late; the magic was gone.

During the day, clouds drift across the sky without much notice given to them. But in the evening, during that comma of time between daylight and darkness, the sun's filtered light paints color onto those clouds, turning them into a kaleidoscopic billboard.

Our minds try to click onto the sunset to recall it later, but the shapes shift with each breath, the colors meld, and the cloudscape falls away as quickly as a dream upon waking.

My brother, Leon, who lives in Alaska, spent two weeks in Kansas this past summer. He photographed the sunsets every evening.

On his blog, Leon suggested that perhaps Kansas could focus less on some of the other state promotions and simply market our skies. "The real money is in sunsets," Leon wrote. "Build motels and restaurants with big west-facing windows, promote them to people from soggy states, and you'll have a moneymaker."

Because we've had so many incredible sunsets this autumn, I wondered if any one season produced more beautiful sunsets than another. So I asked that question of Mark Bogner, meteorologist at KSN-TV in Wichita.

Apparently, each of our four seasons is an equal-opportunity sunset provider.

"We are fortunate," Bogner said, "to get spectacular sunsets year-round from the thunderstorm anvil-cloud sunsets of the spring, to the harvest-dust-colored sunsets of summer, to the Rocky Mountain cirrus sunsets of fall, to the ice pillar sunsets of the winter."

While traveling around the state, I've watched these peach-tangerine-pomegranate sunsets from the Kansas highways. But at home, I tend to miss them. Our house faces east and the view to the west is blocked by trees, houses, garages; i.e., ground clutter. While I am in a good position to catch sunrises, I don't always catch the evening event.

My friend Janet Fish, of Madison, paid close attention to sunsets when she and her husband, Larry, lived in Emporia. She said, "There were late afternoons when Larry would zip in and holler 'sunset alert' and we'd stand in the yard and watch with our arms around each other."

Janet said that from their location the color in the sky would glow behind the steeple of Sacred Heart Church. "Some nights it was so stunning that it would bring tears to our eyes."

Janet has suggested a neighborhood notification system, church bells perhaps, something that would get our attention and send us all out into our yards to take in the show.

I asked Mark Bogner if sunsets could be forecast.

He said, "A fairly reliable forecast of a pretty sunset can be made a few hours in advance by looking at a satellite picture, but the atmosphere is still full of surprises and some set-ups that look great give average sunsets, and occasionally one that looks like it might not bring much will just take your breath away!"

Viewing a fiery Kansas sunset can make us pause, breathe deeply, turn a crazy day into a moment of peace, as that poem of light shifts against the darkening sky.

Our lives would be richer, wouldn't they, if we each spent one minute a day watching the sky fill with flaming color. I can picture it now in every Kansas town: yards, sidewalks and driveways filling with neighbors, heads raised, eyes to the western sky, absorbing that moment of splendor. Let's do it. I'll meet you outside tonight.

# Community

*September 2003*

# OUR FINEST, OUR BRAVEST

September. It's still the same, but it's not quite what it used to be.

Air sparkles when humidity disappears. The skies are postcard blue.

Sunflowers brighten ditches and shades of yellow ochre add depth to green pastures. School has begun. Schedules resume. We put on sweaters and jackets for the Friday night football games.

Two years ago, we had a morning as clean and fresh as sheets breathing on a clothesline. I turned off the *Today Show* and sat at my desk to write. I was impressed with my self-discipline.

But after an hour or so, I grew restless and clicked on the TV. One of the towers of the World Trade Center had fallen, the second soon would. Newsman Tom Brokaw said that the seemingly impenetrable "Fortress America" was under attack.

When Dave came home for lunch, he mentioned the circling contrails he had seen in the sky. Air traffic had been grounded. Instead of the straight-line streaks, the white lines looped, curved, headed for the nearest port, Wichita.

TV news stations dropped all commercials for four days. The news didn't stop coming. I couldn't stop watching.

But during those shock-filled, horrific days, people softened, hearts opened. We began to treasure family, friends, even strangers in a way that we hadn't before.

We were saddened and angered by the killing and maiming of thousands at the Pentagon and in New York City. We recognized bravery in the passengers who challenged the hijackers over Pennsylvania.

We staggered at the loss of 343 firefighters and at least 60 police officers who died at the World Trade Center.

That day, firefighters, police officers and members of the military climbed up the status ladder. We wondered how we could have taken them for granted.

After the recent flash flooding on the Kansas Turnpike south of Emporia, which tore away six human lives, I thought not only of the victims and their families, but also about the rescue personnel.

I thought about the Kansas Highway Patrol troopers who assisted the survivors. I thought about the rescue workers who located the washed-away minivan, the ones who found the bodies of the children, those who continued the search for the missing mother and the man from Texas.

It's unpleasant to imagine the disturbing scenes that rescue workers encounter. So usually, we don't.

We applaud firefighters for running into burning buildings and police officers for arresting criminals. We are well aware of their occupational hazards. We honor them for making rescues, for saving lives and for protecting us from danger.

But I hope that we also appreciate them for the emotional stresses they face, the split-second decisions they have to make, and for handling those disquieting tragedies.

Years ago when I dispatched for the Lyon County Sheriff's Department, I hated the calls of injury accidents. It bothered me that some locations in Lyon County were 20–30 minutes away from an ambulance.

I paced the floor until an officer and the EMTs arrived on the scene. Then, from my perspective, the situation was under control. The injured were receiving the care they needed.

After working an accident, the deputy or trooper often came to the office and talked about the accident scene and the severity of the injuries. But they never spoke about how it made them feel.

I like to think that each of us is on a heroic mission on this planet just by living our lives, doing our jobs and taking care of each other.

But let us keep in mind our collective heroes: our finest, our bravest. When sirens pierce the peaceful air, send good thoughts to the one who is waiting, and whisper a word of thanks to those on the way.

*July 2007*

# FINDING GREG

Front Street looks pretty much the way it did when I was in second grade. I remember well that trip to Dodge City, especially the getting-lost part.

In May, on our way to Colorado, Dave and I stopped in Dodge. We didn't tour Boot Hill, but just seeing Front Street again returned a strong memory. Many years ago, I nearly ended up in the Boot Hill lost-and-found box along with the sad umbrellas and lonely mittens.

Area Lions Clubs had arranged for the Santa Fe Railroad to haul a bunch of kids from across Kansas to Dodge in a passenger train. We were to visit Boot Hill, have a picnic and return the same day.

My dad, who was a Lions Club member, and my brother and I, along with a handful of other hometown kids stood at the Pawnee Rock depot as the train approached from the east.

In Pawnee Rock, we were used to seeing freight trains. They dropped off boxcars which would be loaded with grain from the elevator or pellets from the Cargill Salt Plant. However, that misty morning was the first time I had ever seen a passenger train stop there.

As the locomotive pulled us westbound, every kid on the train had to try walking down the aisle. It felt awkward to move in the same direction as the train and equally odd to head the other way.

The train had a concession stand in one of the cars and, after begging a nickel off Dad, I made my way to it and bought one of those flat, rectangular, orange-and-white slabs of taffy, wrapped in waxed paper.

In Dodge City, our large group wandered through the

various buildings on Front Street.

We entered a gift store, wildly colorful and exciting, with Indian headdresses hanging on wall hooks, along with moccasins, cap guns and low-slung gun belts. A countertop offered marbles and sets of jacks.

When I looked up from the tomahawks and harmonicas, I saw — no Dad, no brother, no one I knew!

Yo-yos and bracelets could wait; I had to find my dad. Adrenaline burned as I searched each face in the room. Strangers, every one.

If I couldn't find my dad or anyone familiar, how would I get back to the train? How would I get home? I was alone in a strange town. With no one to save me, I pictured myself living in an orphanage, eating oatmeal from strange bowls.

Today's youngsters are better connected to the world than we were. They have cell phones and can call home or 9-1-1.

After a few minutes of fear, I found Greg Davidson, a lanky boy from Pawnee Rock. My thoughts of that orphanage dissolved.

Greg was four years older than me, someone I knew, but not very well. He was in sixth grade — practically an adult.

"Can you help me find my dad?" I whimpered, looking up into his kind eyes.

"We'll find him," Greg said, putting his hand on my shoulder and keeping it there as we snaked through the packed room. My dad was somewhere ridiculously close; I had just lost him in the crowd.

Several years ago, I mentioned this incident to Greg when I saw him in Pawnee Rock. He didn't remember it. But I do. And when he crosses my mind, I always smile. Those who treat us kindly are the ones we remember 40 years later.

You never know who's going to save you. Sometimes it's a 12-year-old boy in a plaid shirt and blue jeans.

*April 2013*

# 'LITTLE HOUSE ON THE PRAIRIE'

Every afternoon, Mary Louise Wilhite read to her second-grade students at Pawnee Rock Grade School. Following our after-lunch recess, my classmates and I came in from the playground, windblown and energetic. But we settled down quickly because it was reading time.

Mrs. Wilhite pulled her chair out from behind her desk and placed it in the center of the classroom, to read to us from one of the nine books by Laura Ingalls Wilder. For 15 minutes, nothing was required of us except to be quiet and listen.

Day by day, Mrs. Wilhite led us through the childhood of Laura Ingalls Wilder. My classmates and I took in the adventures of Laura and Mary and Carrie, Ma and Pa, and Jack the dog. We heard about storms and illnesses and daily pioneer life. As Mrs. Wilhite read, we pictured the log cabin and the girls doing their daily chores and helping Ma with the cooking and sewing.

After listening to our teacher read these books in 1967, I read them all myself at least once. Seven years later, in 1974, the *Little House on the Prairie* series began on TV and I had the chance to see Laura and Mary and Carrie grow up all over again.

Now, decades later, I can't say that I remember the details of Laura's stories, but I do remember being a wide-eyed listener in that second-grade classroom.

A few weeks ago, Dave and I were in southern Kansas near Sedan and had some extra time for exploring, so we headed east to check out the historic location of the Ingalls home, which is about 12 miles southwest of Independence.

In the 1960s, research began to determine the exact location of the Ingalls family cabin. Thanks to the presence of Charles Ingalls' hand-dug well, the property was found. In 1977, a replica one-room log cabin was built on the site. It's a tiny dwelling with a couple of windows, and standing inside it's easy to see where the term "cabin fever" comes from. It's very close quarters for a family of five including infant Carrie who was born in Kansas.

The story of the Ingalls family begins in *Little House in the Big Woods,* the book set in Wisconsin where Laura was born in 1867. In 1869, the Ingalls family moved to Kansas and we read about their times here in the third book, *Little House on the Prairie.* In her books, Laura makes herself and her siblings a few years older than they were in real life.

To add more layers of history to the replica cabin, the Sunny-side schoolhouse and the Wayside post office were moved onto the historic site. These two buildings were not in use until after the Ingalls family had left our state, but the structures offer visitors a better sense about the early days in Kansas.

An outhouse is on site and it is also not historic; I was pleased to find that the outhouse had running water and flushable toilets. Also on the property are a few farm animals, as well as the (now sealed) hand-dug well.

It wasn't until I stood in the gift shop and saw a shelf filled with the Laura Ingalls Wilder books that I remembered Mrs. Wilhite reading these books to us. Immediately, I saw myself back in that second-grade classroom, sitting at my desk, leaning into those stories of life on the Kansas prairie a long, long time ago.

*June 2004*

# MARY THE MUSICIAN

It's Vacation Bible School season. Churches around Emporia have signs posted in their yards, inviting children to come to their classes.

I loved Bible school when I was young. My hometown had a community-run weeklong event held in our grade school building.

It was summer so regular classroom rules were relaxed. We blurted answers rather than raising our hands. We talked to our friends without being reprimanded. And we wore shorts, a dress code no-no during regular school days.

My favorite part of Bible school was the music. Now I sing so far out of tune that my notes are beyond flat and sharp; they hover in some alien key. Nevertheless, when Mary Stimatze got the class singing happily and loudly, I couldn't help but join in.

Mary was in charge of the music for Bible school. She was the mother of my good friends, Marilyn and Sarah. Music was their first language. The family was fluent in chords and melodies.

Mary's brother headed a traveling group called Whitey Gleason and the Jubilee Quartet, and some of the songs she taught us were his compositions.

We also sang traditional songs, including "(I've Got that Joy, Joy, Joy, Joy) Down in My Heart."

I'd have to say that one of our favorite songs was "John the Baptist."

The second-to-last line of each stanza asked, "Who was this man?" Instead of always following with, "John the Baptist," we sometimes changed the words to "Bill the fireman." And occasionally, "Bob the butcher."

We weren't trying to be disrespectful; we were 8-year-olds

trying to be funny. Mary understood; she had four (later, five) kids of her own. We were enthusiastic and otherwise well behaved, so she let it slide.

Because she allowed us to have fun, Bible school was, as it should be, joyful.

Mary was also our Girl Scout leader. She started a troop in a tiny town that offered few extracurricular activities for children besides vandalism.

Each week, about a dozen Girl Scouts met in the basement of the Pawnee Rock Methodist Church. We sold cookies, bobbed for apples, made s'mores.

Mary was easygoing but she let us know when we trespassed or went too far.

One summer night in our early teens, Marilyn, Sarah, and a few other friends and I decided to cook a sunrise breakfast at The Rock, the state park on the hill north of town.

I was to bring the eggs and milk for French toast. Debbie said she'd furnish the skillet and matches. Marilyn and Sarah agreed to supply the bread and table service. We made plans to meet at the post office at 5:15 a.m.

In her parting words that evening, Marilyn said, "If we're not at the post office, just come in our house and wake us up."

Well, Marilyn and Sarah weren't at the post office and we didn't really think we should enter their house in the dark and walk up the creaky wooden stairs to the second floor. But, on the other hand, Marilyn had said it was OK.

As it turned out, we didn't have the opportunity to climb those creaky stairs.

The creaky front door gave us away. Mary charged out of her bedroom. She was angry and sent us outside.

Mary was fair. She let Marilyn and Sarah come with us. We enjoyed a sunrise breakfast at The Rock that has become a well-worn memory, even though our French toast was limp and the cookie dough that was brought along didn't bake at all over a puny twig fire.

Now it's another grown-up summer. And every June the Vacation Bible School signs around Emporia remind me of John the Baptist. (And Bill the fireman.)

And I think of Mary, the musician, Girl Scout leader, mother of my friends. I can't imagine a childhood without her.

*December 2008*

# MELLENCAMP'S 'SMALL TOWN'

Eighteen times.

The other day when I heard John Mellencamp's "Small Town" play on the car radio, I counted.

And I ran out of fingers, because he uses the phrase "small town" 18 times, ending most of his lines with those words. It's hard to miss the drift of that song.

Now I realize that he's using repetition for emphasis, but still, a listener (me, for instance) wants to shout at Mellencamp, "Get a thesaurus!"

I sometimes use the technique of repetition myself. But when writing, one tries not to annoy the reader and doesn't overwork any particular word or phrase, giving each one some breathing room.

But in this particular case, with this particular phrase, I do understand Mellencamp. I have struggled with the "small town" battle many times myself.

Because, what else do you call a small town besides a small town? The best alternative I've come up with is community.

In *The Synonym Finder* by J. I. Rodale, I've looked up the words village and hamlet to check for other options. And there I found: community, burg, pueblo, dorp (dorp?), settlement, municipality, jerkwater town and hick town.

Village and hamlet are nice-sounding words. But how many towns in Kansas seem like hamlets to you? Hamlet is a little too cozy, a little too New England for our open topography.

Even village doesn't seem like a Great Plains kind of a word.

And it's better to reuse the same word than to try to force one that sounds awkward, one that doesn't seem compatible with the piece you're writing.

Mellencamp's song wouldn't be the same without using the

phrase "small town." "I was born in a village" just doesn't cut it.

So that's why, like John Mellencamp, I tend to overuse the words "small town" and "community." Nothing else sounds right.

By the way, how small is a small town? Is it 500 residents? 1,000? Fewer than 2,000 people?

About four years ago, Verna Lee Penner of Inman compiled a list of Kansas towns according to population. The numbers have likely shifted, but at that time Kansas had about 335 towns with fewer than 500 people.

Ninety towns had a population between 500 and 1,000; and 80 towns claimed they had between 1,000 and 2,000 residents. Add up the towns with fewer than 2,000 people and Kansas has about 505 of them.

One writer who knows small towns from the ground up is Haven Kimmel. She has published two memoirs about her childhood in the small Indiana town of Mooreland: *A Girl Named Zippy* and *She Got Up off the Couch*.

In the preface of that second memoir, Kimmel describes Mooreland as a "paradise for a child. It was small, flat and entirely knowable."

She wrote, "When I say the town was small, I mean 300 people. I cannot stress this enough." Then she referred to a town of 6,000 as a "wild metropolis."

"Once a woman told me that she had grown up in a small town of 15,000," Kimmel said, "and I was forced to turn my head away from her crazy geographic assessment."

Yes, the term "small town" is relative. It depends on who is talking or who is singing.

I'm thrilled that Mellencamp writes music about small-town America. I wanted to learn about the place he mentions in that song, the place he was born in 1951, the place where he was raised: Seymour, Indiana.

I've been unable to determine the town's population in 1985 when the song was released, but the numbers that I'm finding on the Internet show that Seymour currently has about 19,000 residents.

Small town? Please.

*August 2010*

# THE LUMBERYARD BENCH

When we were kids, my friends and I were bench bums.

Of course, we would've loved to have been beach bums, but beaches are hard to come by in this landlocked state. So, my gang and I hung out at the lumberyard bench in downtown Pawnee Rock.

When the Clutter-Lindas Lumber Co. was still in business (I think it closed in the early '70s), the bench was occupied in the daytime by lumberyard customers, farmers and retired guys mostly, who sat there to catch up on gossip and rainfall amounts.

During the evenings and weekends, the bench was the hangout of pre-teens and teenagers. Even after the lumberyard closed for good, the bench remained.

When I drive into a small Kansas town these days, a downtown bench is one of the things I look for. Some might underestimate the value of a bench, but in a small town, it's not just a place to sit, it's a destination.

A bench is like the community's front porch where adults can sit in twos and threes and share the stories of their days: tomato production, the granddaughter who has just started college, next week's pancake breakfast at the church.

On the bench attached to the front of our lumberyard, sitters could lean against the building. Above was a wide roof which made the bench a fantastic hide-out from summer rains. Two cottonwood trees grew between the sidewalk and the street, so it was a green spot of sorts which provided extra protection from the late afternoon sun. Plus, one of those trees was climbable, which meant additional seating for group conversations.

And best of all, between those two trees was a red water pump. The handle made a hee-haw sound with the up-and-down motion. Fresh, cold well water splashed out of the spout, which was great for cooling off on August days, water fights or just for scooping hands into the stream for a drink.

Our bench was located at the main intersection in town and since the business district was only two blocks long, the bench was in the center of it all. From there we had a panorama of pretty much all that was going on downtown.

On the four corners of that intersection were the lumberyard, the post office, the grocery store, and my dad's woodworking shop. One could see the comings and goings at the Pawnee Rock Dress Shop, Willard's Welding, the self-service laundry and the beauty salon. Down the street, one of the taverns, Betty's Café, was visible, so we could observe who visited Betty for a cold Schlitz.

One might think that hanging out at the bench was just a way of killing time, but it gave us a chance to sit and watch our town in action, to notice things, to pay attention. We knew every resident's car by sight — and by sound. When a stranger pulled into town, we could spot it a block away. We were friendly (well, desperately lonely) and we'd wave to the travelers who drove through town to visit Pawnee Rock State Park.

I enjoyed our spot so much that when I see a small Kansas community without a downtown bench, it seems as if the town has declared, "Move along, there's nothing to see here."

A town is always changing and there's always something to observe, something to learn.

From that one location, we watched the community evolve and change. We monitored daily life, small-town life. There were no big events that happened on Centre Street, but there was a lot of interaction, simple everyday connections. A bench is good for things like that.

*August 2009*

# A SMILE AND A WAVE

At the four-way stop sat a pickup truck with three 20-something occupants. As I turned left in front of this vehicle, the driver waved a big wave out his side window.

My brain initiated its face-recognition program. Nope, I didn't know the guy or the vehicle. I did wave though. Maybe he knew me; maybe he thought I was someone else. Or maybe he was merely trying to get a response.

Trying to get a response, hmm. I smiled as I recalled another waving incident which had occurred on a Kansas highway long ago and far away.

One day when we were 17, my friend Karla and I wanted to see how many waves we could encourage on the eight-mile stretch between Larned and Pawnee Rock.

I was at the wheel, driving Mildred. I had named my car, a blue 1973 Plymouth Valiant, after my third-grade teacher, Mildred Dunavan.

As far as waving goes, that was just something we all did in the tiny town of Pawnee Rock. During our outgoing and obnoxious stages of girlhood, say, at 8, 9, and 10, my friends and I would walk along U.S. Highway 56 on our way to the gas station to buy Super Bubble bubble gum or Zero candy bars. And as cars zipped through town, we'd wave to show travelers that the natives were friendly.

When semis came by, we'd do the one-arm pump, the gesture required to get truckers to blast their air horns. Making a truck driver react provides an incredible feeling of accomplishment to a pre-teen. And his acknowledgment meant that we were not invisible kids living in an invisible little town.

I don't know if the waving habit was merely a custom of the

time (the '60s and '70s) or the place (central Kansas), but I grew up in a culture of general goodwill, which included waving to oncoming cars in town, on dirt roads and on the highway.

Even now, the farther west you travel in Kansas, the more likely you are to encounter people who have a habit of waving. The population is thinner out west and drivers are more likely to assume they know the oncoming vehicle and its occupants — because they probably do. Or maybe western Kansas folks are just friendlier. Or maybe they're simply excited to see another human being on those empty highways.

But things change, and there seems to be less highway waving these days — probably because drivers are talking on their cell phones, which means: 1) they have no free hand, or 2) they're not as lonely and don't need a shot of connection. And waving is all about connection.

On that particular day in 1977, driving from Larned to Pawnee Rock, Karla and I assumed we could get everyone to respond. About one-third of all drivers waved spontaneously anyway, but pretty much everyone would wave in return.

Karla and I raised our hands when the first car drove by. Nothing. The next car, no response.

We got bolder, filling the windshield with our hands. Yet no one waved back. Five cars, six, seven, and not one wave.

A mile or so from Pawnee Rock, the Buick that had been following us since Larned overtook us in the left lane and Karla and I turned to look at the occupants.

In the Buick sat an older man and woman, both smiling, and both waving big waves at us. Then they sped away. Karla and I burst out laughing.

That couple had been observing us; they got it. Then they connected, and they made us laugh. Three decades later I still remember that simple gesture of kindness.

Sometimes all it takes to make someone's day is a smile and a wave.

*April 2011*

# ONE MAN'S LEGACY

The school bus I rode in bounced over a one-lane pasture road. It sloshed through a muddy draw, wound around hills, and stopped near a granite monument in the middle of a Chase County pasture.

More than 200 people made the trip from the Bazaar schoolhouse to the Knute Rockne Memorial on April 2.

We gathered on property owned by Leonard Cornelius for the 80th anniversary commemoration of the plane crash that killed the Notre Dame football coach and seven others on March 31, 1931. Their small plane, en route from Kansas City, Mo., to Los Angeles, lost a wing and fell to the earth.

As we gathered, the sky was blue with a few high clouds. The field around us was covered with scattered rocks and thick dry grass.

The much-beloved Knute Rockne was a Norwegian immigrant who coached the Fighting Irish from 1918 until the time of his death at age 43. He had a 105-12-5 record and three national championships.

Quite a few in the crowd had ties to Notre Dame. Out on the open pasture, "Here Come the Irish" played over the speakers. Nils Rockne, one of Knute's grandsons, told stories about his grandfather.

At 10:48 a.m., the reported time of the 1931 crash, local resident Doug Wilson buzzed in for a flyover in his red, white and blue airplane. The plane rose dramatically in altitude over the site, then circled around and away. A bagpiper played "Amazing Grace."

But the event was not all about Knute Rockne or the other victims. Much love and appreciation was extended to the memory of the man who took care of this spot for decades, the late Easter Heathman.

At age 13, Heathman came with his father to this location on that spring day in 1931. During his adult years, he returned to the site countless times with visitors, many of whom were Notre Dame folks making a pilgrimage to see where Rockne's life had ended.

Easter Heathman was a World War II veteran and a local farmer. Because he was an eyewitness to the event, at some point people started coming to his door. He would take them to the site and share his memories of the day the plane went down.

Heathman died in 2008 at age 90. I never met him, but I wish I had. From the accounts I heard, he was a kind and generous man, and he faithfully tended to the crash site without fanfare and helped organize memorial events.

Over the years, a connection grew between Heathman and Notre Dame. In 2006, the Notre Dame Monogram Club paid tribute to Heathman with an honorary monogram. Posthumously, in 2009, a plaque recognizing Heathman's dedication to the Rockne crash site was created and placed at the Notre Dame football stadium.

At this recent service, Nils Rockne, Knute Rockne's grandson, expressed appreciation on behalf of his family for Heathman's "unselfish devotion." Rockne said, "He simply did it because he loved my grandfather for who he was and what he stood for."

Heathman was a farmer, but his second calling was to honor the eight men who died on that pasture near Bazaar. His devotion to the crash site memorial deeply touched the victims' families as well as the Notre Dame folks who loved Knute Rockne and his legacy.

What matters most in this world is how we connect with others, how we give of ourselves. In helping to keep the memory of Knute Rockne alive, Easter Heathman created his own legacy — one of love, of generosity, of devotion.

*May 2003*

# REMEMBERING THE DEAD

The cemetery was my playground.

While Dad mowed, my 6-year-old self blew fluff off of dandelions. I traced the engraving on stones, and I climbed into the arms of a cedar tree and watched ants scatter as I peeled its hairy bark.

My dad was the sexton of the Pawnee Rock Township Cemetery. A windy hill, just north of the city limits, was where we kept the town's departed.

This was the family business. Dad rode the mower while Mom and my brother, Leon, and I trimmed the buffalo grass near the stones with hand clippers. I worked in the cemetery each year until I left for college in 1977.

When I was a child, the carved names were merely names. But now, many of the newer stones represent people I once knew.

Under the shadow of cedars toward the cemetery's north end lies Harry Lewis, a bachelor, retired from the U.S. Railway Postal Service. He kept to himself mostly, didn't speak to kids, and he wore a city man's hat.

One Halloween, my friends and I dared ourselves to trick-or-treat at Harry Lewis' home, doubting he'd open his door, afraid that he would. Harry answered, then stepped away into the darkness of his house. He returned with foil-wrapped cylinders, peeled back the aluminum and handed us each a nickel.

My third-grade teacher, Mildred Dunavan, rests on the east side of the cemetery. When I got my first car, a 1973 Plymouth Valiant, I named the car Mildred in her honor.

Aunt Juletha and Uncle Herman are on the west side, neighbors to U.S. Senator George McGill, a 1930s Democrat, perhaps the most famous of the residents here.

Another grave nearby belongs to Carole Mead, the mother of my friend Karla. Carole drove me to the Larned hospital the day I broke my arm during an eighth-grade mishap. She always had a grin and a punch line. With Carole gone, the world is missing a bit of its orneriness.

Stones from the late 1800s, speckled white-yellow-green with lichens, huddle near the graveyard's entrance on the south side. One of my great-great-grandfathers is buried here under a narrow, vertical stone with an inscription "Born in Russia."

Memorial Day is the big day in the cemetery world. For weeks in advance, we spent long days perfecting the acreage, trimming tree limbs, cutting grass, hoping to add beauty and order to the emotion of remembrance.

Several days before the holiday, while we did the final touch-up work, the pebble-covered roads filled with Chevrolets and Fords and Buicks.

Visitors left bouquets of white and pink peonies in coffee cans, weighted with sand and water. Crosses made of red plastic carnations marked graves like exclamation points. Daisies in Hellmann's mayonnaise jars were held steady in the wind with wire cut from clothes hangers, one end bent over the lip of the glass, the other end speared into the soil.

A visitor might place his hand on top of a headstone, a pause before he turned toward his car. We would look away, ashamed to have intruded on a private moment.

By Memorial Day, the cemetery danced with life and color. Small American flags flapped over the graves of military veterans.

About a week later, we returned for the cleanup. We plucked the Hellmann's jars, pouring the water, now thick and green, onto the roadway. We tossed the cans and browned peonies into the bed of Dad's truck. Plastic flowers were moved close to the stones where they wouldn't be caught by the mower.

Lives pass. Memorial Day comes and goes. A story, a bond, a kindness: these things remain.

*March 2013*

# REMEMBERING ADAM

"When we got here, we went out to look at the farm," Amy said with a smile. "That's what Dad would've done."

Amy's father, Adam Deckert, had passed away at age 94. I've been friends with Amy for the complete length of my memory. She now lives in Lenexa, but back in the day, Amy lived two-and-a-half oft-traveled blocks from my home in Pawnee Rock. We both belonged to the Mennonite church, and as the only girls in our Sunday school class, we became fast friends.

I spent almost as much time at Amy's house as I spent at my own, and Adam and Helen were like a second set of parents to me. Helen, who died in 1996, was a busy housewife, the mother of six (one of whom died in childhood). The older kids, Anna Sue, Frances and Howard, occasionally babysat for me and my brother. Ida is Leon's age, and Amy is a year younger than me.

When someone we know passes from this world, we spend time in thought, pondering the impact they've had on us, how their existence has helped shape our lives. And what came to mind about Adam was that he was a kind soul, and that he was always simply "there." He was present for his family and he was present for me.

Adam taught Amy and me how to play pinochle, and he played Monopoly with us. When the Deckerts purchased a ping-pong table, Amy and I took on Adam, two against one, and tried to beat him, but he was pretty good.

During blizzards, Adam and Helen let us turn the living room into a fort for days at a time. We stretched quilts and blankets across furniture, securing the blanket ends with stacks of books.

Adam had been a weekend farmer, raising wheat and milo

on land near my grandmother's farm. One spring evening in the '60s, Adam took Amy and me out to check on his crop. The ripening wheat was nearly as tall as we were. Adam warned us against trampling the stalks as Amy and I disappeared into the field to play hide-and-seek.

Adam's full-time job was at the Pawnee Rock Salt Plant just north of town. When he left the salt plant, he took a soldering job at Doerr's Metal Products in Larned, where he helped make livestock tanks.

He loved to share riddles and puzzles. He made sure his kids had piano lessons, and he enjoyed going to their recitals. Adam memorized poetry and had at least an hour's worth of recitation he could perform. At church picnics, Adam would be one of the first to get the game of horseshoes going.

Adam was tall and he was thin all of his life. He was a good listener and not one to argue. He was a gentle man, a quiet man, a man of peace. In the eulogy written by his children, they said that Adam never picked a fight, but that he would be there to defend someone else. And he was one of many fine folks in our church who fully embodied the Mennonite spirit of helping those in need.

I was always happy to be invited to tag along with the Deckerts to Sunday after-church dinners with their extended family. Amy and I were inseparable during those years, and Adam and Helen treated me like one of their own. A kid couldn't ask for a better deal than that.

*June 2013*

# DEATH OF A CHURCH

Every Sunday morning during my childhood, as the ushers carried the collection plates to the altar, we stood to sing "Praise God from Whom All Blessings Flow."

A few weeks ago, when the congregation of my hometown church began the song, tears filled my eyes. I knew it would be the last time I heard it sung in that building.

"If it feels as if you've come to a funeral today, well you have, kind of," Pastor Lynn Schlosser said as she began her sermon.

In the 1870s, hundreds of German Mennonites immigrated to Kansas from Russia. A group of 21 families settled in Barton County, and in 1875 they began the Bergthal Mennonite Church. Among them were my father's ancestors.

1915 is the imprint on the cornerstone of this red-brick church three miles north of Pawnee Rock. Soon, this structure will be dismantled. A leaky roof caused mold to grow in the basement. An abandoned church would either cave in over time or be subject to cruel vandalism. Watching that decay would be doubly tragic, so the congregation decided to have the church demolished.

Rural depopulation has dropped the attendance to about 14 on any given Sunday. While this church once represented a large farming community, many of the family farms — and the families themselves — have disappeared. Kids, like me, went off to college and started lives elsewhere. Church elders have passed on.

I knew these folks to be kind people, dedicated to service. They were sturdy and stoic Germans who didn't waste resources or words. And they held to their principles; you were unlikely to see a farmer cutting wheat on a Sunday afternoon although his crop might be ruined by that evening's storm.

Each Sunday morning my family pulled into the church's sand-and-sticker parking lot. As a youngster in Sunday school, my classmates and I drew maps of the travels of Jesus. During sermons my friend Amy and I played tic-tac-toe in the margins of the church bulletins. At 14, we were baptized, sprinkled with water — the Mennonite way.

On this recent Memorial Day Sunday, the church was packed. Stained-glass windows were raised to let in the gusty wind, a constant on this hill. Families reunited — brothers, sisters, aunts, uncles, cousins. The Mennonites had come to say goodbye to the building.

Pastor Schlosser said, "I am thankful so many of you have come home one more time to this people, this place, this church, to tell her how much you have loved her and how much she has meant to you."

She said, "Two and a half years ago, rather than to deny the church's condition any longer, we faced reality and acknowledged the condition was terminal, and began a really emotional journey preparing for the end while simultaneously working to live and serve fully throughout our final years.

"I promise you, Bergthal will live on, does live on, in a myriad of mysterious and holy ways," Rev. Schlosser said.

"We've dealt with such a mix of emotions these last few years: grief, anger, shame, disappointment, relief, confusion.

"Surely we've let all these good people who labored hard to build this church, surely we've let them down."

She said, "We see through a mirror but dimly. But if we listen closely, we might just hear their voices raised in a song of triumph. I believe they stand together this day, singing a song of hope and faith. They see what we can only intuit."

Soon this house of worship will be taken down with due respect. These good people created such a strong foundation for my life. And *that* is a church that cannot be dismantled.

*Ordinary Time*

*March 2011*

# THE GOLDEN HOUR

As I write this, Emporia sits under a clear sky. Cobalt blue stretches from one horizon to the other: 180 degrees of happiness. It feels good, especially since we've spent the last few days in a cold, damp gloom.

Although some days the sun can't claw its way through a thick sky, we often have abundant sunshine. Less brilliant, but just as delightful, are moonlight and starlight.

But of all the celestial offerings, there are two hours of light that may be the most profound — the hour after sunrise and the hour before sunset. This luminous glow doesn't occur every day but when it does, the Kansas landscape wears its Sunday best.

This particular quality of illumination makes everything look good. And this is not just ordinary evening light I'm talking about — it's the cleanest and clearest of light, glimmering and charismatic. When this light is cast, even power poles shine like grinning children. It turns dilapidated farm buildings into glowing shrines.

One February evening as Dave and I were driving home from Salina, the sun let loose with a carpet-roll of tingly light. We were southbound on a county road; the sun's rays streamed from the west and every tall weed stood in the spotlight. Each plant shimmered as if it were the belle of the ball, dressed in its finest garb.

"It brings out the dimensionality of things," Dave said when I asked him how he, as a photographer, perceives this light. "The lighting from the side brings out form and texture. It sculpts the hills."

When you throw a small, flat rock across a lake at a proper angle, it skips, skimming the surface of the water. And that's what this light does, too, because it's coming in at such an angle to the earth. It hits on the hills and sends low spots into the shadows.

Last August, my mother and brother and I took a drive in Stafford County. It was one of those evenings of enchanting light. Everything was defined and incandescent. It was as if I couldn't take a bad photograph. On a road thick with sand, that sand shimmered. The Radium elevator was radiant.

Meteorologist Mark Bogner of KSN-TV in Wichita gave me an explanation of this quality of light: "The sun is shining through much more of the atmosphere at those lower angles, thus more of it is filtered, scattered and reflected, giving it a different 'temperature color' and overall tone."

Once, as I was traveling eastbound through Rice County, the evening sun spread its love over a wheat field. I could barely stand the intensity of golden light on golden grain.

I pulled off of the highway onto a dirt road, stepped from my car and gazed in awe at a magical kingdom. Everything glowed; the sun's angle lit clouds from below. The power of the view swelled inside my chest; tears came to my eyes.

This particular quality of light is palpable — it vibrates in your body. This cast of light is fresh and clean and, in a strange way, offers clarity of inner vision as well as outer vision. In one bright moment you can feel absolutely and totally connected with the world.

Because Kansas sunsets are so gorgeous, we are often tricked into looking only to the west. But, as the sun tilts toward the horizon and approaches landfall, take a turn to the east and see your world in a whole new light.

*March 2012*

# TWO GIRLS, TULIPS AND RAINBOWS

Sitting in the March sun feels pretty much like falling in love. The chill of winter is gone and that sweet warm sun makes my skin smile. Birds, unseen, chirp in the trees around me. Cars drive past, a lone bicyclist coasts by.

Daffodils are spent, but grape hyacinths and the forsythia are in bloom. In front of the porch is a small circle of tulips, their blossoms lipstick red.

Taryn, a neighbor girl who has since moved away, sold us the tulip bulbs years ago during a school fundraiser. I think of Taryn each spring as tulip foliage pushes itself out of the brown earth. It grows fast, surely an inch a day. Buds appear and the flowers open with the first red splash of the season.

For the past 15 years, as the seasons have changed, as the earth has orbited the sun again and again and again, I've spent time on this front porch. From here I've watched neighbors move in, neighbors move out.

During the same month that Dave and I purchased our home, the McCoys moved in next door and they promptly celebrated Taryn's first birthday. Two years after that, Morgan was born. The McCoys were great neighbors, the kind of folks from whom you could borrow a piece of aluminum foil when baking, or a lawn edger when your grass crept over the sidewalk.

On Taryn's first day of kindergarten, she and Brenda stopped as they walked home from school, and I asked Taryn, "What did you learn today?" She said, "I learned to keep my hands to myself."

Several years ago, Dave gave me a lighted hula hoop for my birthday. One night after dark, 9-year-old Morgan and I took turns with that hula hoop in our front yard. Dave's photos captured flashes of blue, yellow, red and green swirling around us like lightning bugs.

One morning in 2005, Brenda rang the doorbell, and with a bit of panic in her voice said, "Please tell me that both of your cats are indoors." They weren't, and yes, that was our Bear lying in the street. I placed him in a cardboard box and carried him to the porch. Brenda and I sat on the steps, her arm around me, tears falling on Bear's soft gray fur.

One spring evening after a thunderstorm, Morgan came to the door with her usual bright-eyed smile and said, "There's a rainbow. I thought you'd like to see it." Well, of course we did.

And that became a tradition after storms: a knock on the door followed by a neighborhood viewing of the rainbow.

In 2008, Tyson eliminated its slaughter operations and dramatically cut its workforce. Both John and Brenda worked at Tyson. Brenda still had her job in the office, but John's position was cut. After several anxious months, John found employment in Kansas City. We didn't want them to move and they didn't want to either.

"All of my life I've wanted to leave this town," John said. "And now that I have to, I don't want to go."

The moving van came and went. They are settled in the city and are happy there. But we miss them. We miss John and Brenda, and we miss those two girls with wavy brown hair who rode their bikes up and down the sidewalk, the girls who loved to laugh and tell stories, the girls who were never without a question.

The tulips are blooming now, and in the rainy days ahead, the sun will surely project a rainbow or two onto the sky. Dave and I have to discover rainbows on our own these days, but for a few shining moments, there was a sweet young girl who led us to them.

*April 2012*

# HOME HAS ARRIVED

Green is back.

While driving on Prairie Street the other day, I looked at the baby green leaves cutting a colorful new skyline against the background of blue. And one word came to mind: home.

Spring returns us to the green that I have craved since October, when bug-eaten leaves turned yellow or red or brown and fell to earth.

For me, spring is home. Spring pushes fresh air into my lungs; its delicious warmth settles into my bones. Spring helps me see things in the clearest of light.

Home is one of the most soothing words in our language. It suggests a place where you can be yourself, truly and completely. A dozen situations of "home" popped into my head. Home was giggling with childhood friends and exploring my grandmother's farm.

I thought of the hiding places I had in my childhood backyard: under the lilac bushes, behind the pussy willow and up in the silver lace vine, which created its own foliage hammock between the evergreens and the fence along the alley.

Home is being with my mother. When I visit her in Arkansas, I'll sit on her couch, around me a circle of books that I've pulled from her shelves. While I read, she works a crossword puzzle in the recliner.

Home is staying in my mom's guest room; it's that softer-than-Kansas air washing through the window screen as I fall asleep. In the morning I wake to the calls of forest songbirds.

In this one grand life, we each discover our own pockets of home. And when the world feels like it is burning at both ends, when we walk down the gangplanks of tough days at work, we can escape into our minds, run back to our hiding places under the lilac bushes or climb into that hammock of silver lace.

Our lives are a broken timeline. We can skip around through our past, finding memories that feel like home. Some of us remember collecting baseball cards, and listening to night games of the Royals on a transistor radio, the voice under our pillow announcing that Freddie Patek had stolen another base.

Memory repositories are like the water table. Those memories seem to drop, fade over time. But when the rains come, the water table rises, allowing those comforting memories to return.

Home for some of us was playing a Triple Word Score in the evenings at the dining room table. When the letter C clattered onto the linoleum floor, the dog rushed over to sniff it, hoping that the C would spell "cheese," her favorite food.

Maybe we feel at home while baking our grandmother's pumpkin pie recipe, or enjoying dinner with our spouse. Home might be keeping the spine straight, writing down our stories, making room for all of our shadows.

Perhaps home is waking before dawn and stepping outside where the night sky lingers with stars and deep indigo.

Our lives reflect a complicated geography of where we've been and where we hope to go. Our lives are like vast prairies and endless skies.

And right now, in Kansas, we have green grass on the ground and green leaves in the air. Home has arrived.

*December 2012*

# TRACY'S HOMETOWN

If Tracy and I had grown up in the same town during the same time period, I'll bet we would have been childhood friends.

A few weeks ago, I traveled with Tracy Simmons to her hometown of Dodge City for an overnight visit. She gave me the native's tour of the town and of her rural neighborhood.

Many of you may know Tracy; she's the manager of the Emporia Farmers Market. She's also a writer — and it was on the level of writing that she and I first connected.

Raised on a farm near Dodge City, she and three siblings grew up with fabulous sunsets, a steady wind and a horse or two in the pasture; cousins lived in the house down the road.

I've always enjoyed hearing Tracy's memories from Dodge. I've heard about her farm, have seen a few photographs, and so it was fun for me to visit some of Tracy's favorite places, to be on a narrated tour with the owner of those stories.

Walking around downtown Dodge City, Tracy showed me the closed Dodge Theater with its now-sagging marquee. Tracy had her own fond memories of the theater, but it holds a bit of family history too. "My mom had her first job here as a ticket-taker," Tracy said. Later, at her dad's house, she showed me a 1955 photograph of her late mother wearing her usherette uniform.

We drove past the old high school (now the middle school) and her grade school, Sunnyside. She showed me where her mother had worked and pointed out a building down the street to which she had often walked to purchase comic books. I thought: this could've been my life.

Near Tracy's house is her church's cemetery, where her mom was buried in 1997. Many of Tracy's stories over the years have been about her mother.

As we walked among the gravestones, Tracy knew the names, the families, their stories, their tragedies. Growing up in a small community, the roots you grow are deep ones.

Tracy and I spent the night at her childhood home where her father and his wife still live, so I got to see this two-story farmhouse of hers. I now had the visual setting for the stories Tracy shared.

When we left her house the next morning, in the adjacent section of land she pointed to the south, "See those two trees over there? That's where I'd go when I ran away from home," Tracy smiled. "I'd pack a suitcase and spend all day there reading a book."

She told me about when she and her cousins took risks playing on thin ice, and also about when they used the barn roof as a slippery slide and the neighbor called her mom to rat on them. She told me of the time her horse unexpectedly reared up, tossed her off and then landed on top of her.

Horses aside, Tracy's childhood adventures were a lot like mine — exploring, reading, and testing the boundaries of parental supervision.

Going to Dodge City with Tracy was like seeing the blueprint for her life. I saw how she became who she is, and, in effect, why we became friends. We have so much common ground, past and present, plus, heck, she's just a fine human being.

I've been in her house and have met her family of origin, so now whenever Tracy tells me a story from her childhood, the setting, the scenery and the characters will all be in place.

*December 2012*

# TUMBLING TUMBLEWEEDS

Just as many of us like to roam across Kansas, Russian thistles, too, are full of wanderlust.

I don't think about tumbleweeds often, but was reminded of them on a recent trip to Dodge City with my friend Tracy Simmons. Russian thistles thrive in the western half of the state; they grow like weeds there. Apparently it takes a lot of space and fresh air to raise these things.

"I miss tumbleweeds," I told Tracy when we first encountered them near Cullison in Pratt County.

"When tumbleweeds blow across the fields, they look like animals moving," Tracy said.

I imagine that tumbleweeds often bounce for miles, crossing property and jurisdiction lines. Maybe we could tag some of these tumblers and see just how far they do venture from their source.

But the lives of tumbleweeds can get cut short. With no road-crossing skills, they may wind up under the brutal tires of a Kenworth, or get caught in the undercarriage of a Camry and scrape the highway for the next 13 miles. Many tumbleweeds are snagged by barbed-wire fences, where they remain imprisoned until they dissolve into the dust from which they came.

Gypsy-like by nature, it's not surprising that these thistles came from Russia and ended up in America's plains states. Windy and arid land is their natural habitat.

Michael John Haddock, author of *Wildflowers and Grasses of Kansas: A Field Guide*, describes them as such: "Russian thistle is a prolific seed producer. The stems break at ground level and roll in the wind causing the seeds to fall. Thus the common name tumbleweed. The seeds require only limited moisture to germinate."

They smuggled themselves across the ocean. Haddock wrote that the thistle was "thought to have arrived in the Great Plains in the mid 1870s with flaxseed imported from Russia."

Tumbleweeds are ours now.

It was a warm November day, in the mid-50s, and Tracy and I drove through strong crosswinds. Wind speed is relative, though; it may not have been overly windy according to western Kansas standards. Dodge City enjoys an average annual wind speed of 13.9 mph and is high on the list of windiest cities in the contiguous United States.

Having grown up with the wind and tumbleweeds in Barton County, I may miss the companionship of these rolling weeds, but I sure don't miss the nagging wind.

The wind blasted us from the south, steady at 30 mph and gusting even stronger. Windbreaks came in the way of semi-trucks traveling in the opposite direction. When an eastbound truck passed us, it blocked the south wind momentarily, pulling the car dangerously toward the center line. But the suction was brief. When the truck passed, the wind returned, pushing the car toward the ditch. It was a two-hands-on-the-steering-wheel kind of a day.

We are warned in the case of flash flooding that two feet of water can float a vehicle, but we are never told about dramatic wind currents, which can also float your car across the highway.

Wind is an invisible element, and it's something of a daily hymn in the western half of Kansas. You cannot see the wind, but neither can you miss its presence. It can slam car doors shut or push an old barn to the ground. And it's the worst hairstylist ever.

But, wind has a purpose: The tumbleweed would be nothing without the wind beneath its wings.

*June 2009*

# BRAVING A REUNION

When Rick, a former grade school classmate, found me via the Internet last summer, he suggested that we locate the others and have a class reunion.

At first I was excited. Then my enthusiasm waned — reunions can be awkward. After a 35-year separation, would we have anything to talk about for more than an hour? Even though I had loved those grade school days, it might be best to preserve my memories as they were, perfect and self-contained.

Our Class of '77 began in the fall of 1964 when 25 little Pawnee Rock punks started kindergarten together. Over the next decade, our class size hovered around 19 or 20. Some kids moved away but others moved in, and we traveled through the years as a team.

Pawnee Rock High School closed and the Class of '72 was the last group of Braves to graduate. My classmates and I hung around through ninth grade, and then in 1974 we split up, attending schools in Macksville, Larned, Otis-Bison and Great Bend.

Eleven of us attended this class reunion on May 23 and we were given the incredible opportunity to tour the Pawnee Rock school building, which is presently owned by a bank.

We took up where we had left off: laughing. We were 14 again. As my friends and I walked down the hallways and stepped into the classrooms, the lunchroom, the gym, our stories poured like a summer rain.

We recalled the red and green cardboard "bricks" in kindergarten. Girls built houses and the boys plowed them down. Standing in a grade school classroom, we paid tribute to Mrs. Schmidt, our vocal music teacher, by singing a few lines from

"Señor Don Gato."

As we surveyed the lunchroom, Darla, a slow eater who tried her best not to get in trouble, said, "Don't ever make the mistake of hiding food in your milk carton."

"Remember Mrs. Latas and her cottage cheese?" Marilyn asked, referring to our sixth-grade teacher. "She brought cottage cheese every day for lunch — and she'd pour ketchup in it."

In sixth grade we watched films (separately, boys and girls) about the facts of life. On the first day of seventh grade our teacher showed us a paddle; it turned out that he wasn't afraid to use it. Another teacher's punishment was for us to hand-copy pages of the *Congressional Record*.

In ninth grade, we baked bread, read "Romeo and Juliet" and learned how to parallel park.

Over the years we had pledged allegiance to the flag, tagged each other in pom-pom-pull-away and learned to play trumpets, saxophones and drums.

We were good kids but did not always present our best selves. Sometimes we were unkind to one another, and naturally we tested our teachers, learning their limits of good cheer.

"Now, what teacher in his right mind would tell his junior high students that he was afraid of snakes?" Jeanette asked.

It felt good to be in the presence of people who had known me even before Mrs. Franklin taught us addition facts. And my classmates hadn't changed much in the past 35 years — their personalities, gestures and ease of laughter had remained the same.

It was after that tour, after we recalled the aroma of homemade rolls in the lunchroom, after we looked for "the ghost in the band room," that I realized that this class reunion had turned into one of the happiest days of my life.

During our grade school years, we spent about 1,800 days in each other's company. And somewhere along the line, our lives melded.

We were just small-town kids, negotiating our way through childhood, together.

*February 2012*

# LOCKED OUT

I turned my back on my car the other day and it locked itself. I heard the click. Luckily, I hadn't left the key somewhere inside the car.

My car has a remote control to lock and unlock its doors, a wonderfully convenient tool, but the car sometimes has its own sneaky agenda.

In general, lockouts don't seem to happen as often as they once did. When I was a new driver in the '70s, it seemed as if every day I saw someone with a metal clothes hanger, untwisting its neck, reaching it into the car, angling it just so, trying to lift the lock knob. In fact, during my teenage years I carried a clothes hanger in my trunk to help friends break into their cars.

Oddly enough, back then when people locked the keys in their car, it was not because they *forgot* to pull the keys from the ignition, but because they accidentally pushed the lock down as they closed the door. People left keys in their cars all the time back then.

Locking the car seemed unnecessary. There was usually nothing in there worth stealing, and theft was a rare event. But the arrival of eight-track players and nice stereo systems got the ball rolling on auto burglaries.

If you did lock your keys in your car, it was a fairly easy problem to resolve. Those were the days of wing windows and lock knobs. If the wing window was open or at least unlocked, you could just reach your arm into the car and lift the lock.

If the wing window was locked, the rubber seal around the main window was pliable and you could slip the clothes hanger in, wiggle it over to the lock knob on the top ledge of the door, catch the knob's lip with the hook and raise it.

Younger readers may not remember wing windows at all. Car windows for front-seat occupants were once divided. The back section rolled down while the front piece was a triangle of glass that swiveled open to let air enter the car sideways. Wing windows provided a gentle air flow.

Once car burglaries became frequent, car makers first did away with the lip on the lock knobs and later integrated the door locks into the door panel.

And it may still be possible to unlock a car using a metal clothes hanger slipped into the door panel; I'm not sure. I've never had a reason to try.

But apparently others have. I was amused a while back when a college-age guy locked the keys in his car in front of my house. It apparently happened during a nighttime party he attended at the house across the street from me.

From my writing desk one morning, I noticed an unfamiliar car parked along the street. Midmorning, this young man drove up and parked behind the first car, got out and peered through the car's window. He tried all the doors and then he drove off.

A little bit later, he returned. This time when he got out of the car, he had a clothes hanger in his hand. Now, I'm sure he got advice to the effect, "All you have to do is slip a clothes hanger down alongside the window, into the door panel, and jimmy the lock."

And that might have worked, except that he had in his hands one of those newfangled thick plastic clothes hangers. Sometimes valuable information, such as how to break into vehicles, skips a generation. Before I could get out there to offer assistance, he took his broken clothes hanger and left.

*April 2003*

# A DAY WITHOUT SUNSHINE

On a Sunday several weeks ago, my husband and I took three separate walks. It was a beautiful spring day, but mostly we just needed to get out of our empty house.

As we walked, we carried the heavy stone of grief. The day before, Dave and I had made the heartbreaking and somewhat sudden decision to have our cat euthanized. Sonny was 12 years old and sick. Until that Friday and an X-ray at the vet's office, we hadn't realized just how sick he was.

Some pets are just pets, but some of them make such an impression that you know you'll remember its personality for the rest of your life. Out of a dozen dogs and cats that I've owned and loved, one dog and this cat have achieved this level of storied family reverence.

Before I met Dave, I adopted Sonny. When the kitten joined me during the dark of winter, I named him Sunshine. Sonny's eyes were outlined in black, and his short hair was variegated gray and black.

As that kitten climbed up the back of my couch and glanced an eye at the tapestry hanging above him, I knew I had a curtain-climber on my hands. I had him neutered and had his front paws declawed.

One day when he was about 6 months old, Sunshine led me to the only tree on the property. He climbed his way to the first branch on the tree, then turned to make sure I had been watching. "See what I can do?" he bragged with his eyes.

Even without claws, he hunted. Sonny deposited dead birds and an occasional baby bunny at our doorstep. Speed was on his side.

Sonny was a runt, with a fighting weight of only 8 pounds,

but he stood his ground. He fought the big cats and became very familiar with (but not fond of) "pink stuff," amoxicillin, for infected wounds.

My cat often showed disgust toward company, so few people understood how he charmed me. Sonny sprawled on the top of the couch and placed his paws on my shoulders as I read, bringing to mind that John Denver song, "Sunshine on My Shoulders."

The cat greeted Dave at the sidewalk each time Dave arrived home. And Sonny expected the same. Upon entering the house, Sonny paused to be petted.

When our "armpit cat" cuddled in for the night, between my torso and my left arm, he put a front paw on my neck to feel my heartbeat.

Sonny trusted us to take care of him and unfortunately it fell to us to determine the hour of his death. How does one decide at what point there is no hope? Or that misery outweighs possibility? How could I, his protector, be the one to say, "Sorry, sweet baby kitten, this is all the time you get?"

His 8-pound body had gradually diminished. During his last night, as he slept in my armpit, I knew that there was no fight left in him.

Dr. Stan Perry was kind and empathetic, and he made sure that Sonny's last moments were painless.

Dave dug a hole in the backyard daylily patch and I turned the soft furry body into the grave. With Sonny, I included a few fluffs of bunny hair (left over from one of his last meals), and some daffodils.

One of Dave's coworkers, Fred, has e-mailed photos of a litter and we might take two of those kittens. The photos show newly opened eyes and fists of razor-sharp claws. Neither of them will be Sunshine, but I'm sure they'll bring their own kind of light.

*August 2006*

# THE DARK SIDE OF OKLAHOMA

You may be wondering why nearly all of my columns are about Kansas.

I never leave the state, that's why.

My stuck-in-Kansas status changed recently when I jumped the border. As dusk lowered the shades on a Saturday evening, I slipped into Oklahoma.

This wasn't exactly a vacation; my mother was sick. An hour after talking with her on the phone, I buckled my seatbelt and aimed the car for Arkansas.

When I left Emporia, I headed east on Interstate Highway 35, then south on U.S. Highway 75 through Burlington, Yates Center, Neodesha, Independence and Caney.

Just outside Caney, I passed that sad yet hopeful white-on-blue highway sign: "Leaving Kansas, Come Again."

Because I had departed Emporia in the early evening, the sun angled sharply from the west. I turned on my headlights.

Mom's illness was serious but not critical, so I was still able to enjoy the ride. I do appreciate the adventure of traveling alone — just me and my car, the hum of tires, the chance to sing along with the radio.

As far as music goes, CDs have their place, but I prefer the radio. I want to hear live voices announce the music. Most of all, I like to be surprised by the next song that the deejay plays.

For instance, it had been decades since I'd last heard Charlie Rich's "The Most Beautiful Girl." OK, now that's not my favorite song or anything, but it made me wonder, whatever happened to Charlie Rich?

The downside to radio is that it's not easy to find a good station. And when you do, the antenna isn't long enough — you can outdrive the signal's range before the end of a song.

An eerie Moody Blues song set the tone for driving through Oklahoma in the dark. The empty highway suddenly seemed a little spooky. Blackness reached outward toward the edges of the earth. I half expected to see a swarm of UFOs congregate over a pasture.

But no UFOs appeared before my windshield. Only Tulsa.

Now, Tulsa is one of my least favorite places to drive through. At night, however, it was a breeze. Under the streetlights, I easily navigated the interchanges. One road sign proclaimed: "America's Most Beautiful Cities — Broken Arrow and Tulsa."

All I can say is that Tulsa didn't look too bad in the dark.

Tired and only halfway to Hot Springs, Ark., I found a motel in Muskogee, a city forever linked to that song. (You know the one.)

(Just curious — why is it that in motel bathrooms the fan and the light are always on the same switch? Sometimes a person, namely me, wants only the light, not a noisy fan.)

I awakened at 4 a.m. and hit the road, leaving the 5:30 wake-up call to ring in an empty room.

While driving at night, all the roads seem flat; there's no texture, no color. You lose your sense of time and distance.

At the Arkansas line, I found a sunrise.

I don't know what to tell you — on my return trip, Oklahoma was still in the dark, from beginning to end.

I'm not too worried about it, though. Just because I didn't see the sun shine on Oklahoma doesn't mean that it doesn't ever happen.

*August 2013*

# WHERE THE HIGHWAY ENDS

In the summer of 1965, my parents took my brother and me to the Arkansas River, a mile south of Pawnee Rock, to see the flood. Heavy rains in Colorado had sent a crash of water downstream.

This was a mighty flood; it washed away the river's wooden bridge. Mingling with other locals, my family stood at the jagged edge of pavement and gaped at the brown water rolling past. We were there as witnesses to one of Pawnee Rock's historic events.

The bridge was missing and the road was broken. This was all rather startling I suppose, but my 6-year-old self was more dazzled by the fact that a boy in my class, Tracy Bright, was wearing a pair of red-framed toy sunglasses just like the pair I had on. The same sunglasses!

Now, decades later in another town, I find myself again standing before a river in flood stage. Over recent weeks, hundreds of Emporians have trekked to the edge of town to view the Cottonwood River. As Kansans, we're always amazed to see water in a hurry to get anywhere. Our streams tend to be small, slow and shallow.

The Cottonwood River filled after heavy rains at the end of July and the beginning of August. Even though the river was expanding out of its banks, it was still rising, until it almost reached the bottom of the old arch bridge.

The new bridge was constructed in 1987, but the 1923 Rainbow Marsh Arch Bridge was preserved for fishermen and for pedestrian traffic. Saving that original bridge was a wise decision. It's a destination. We take visitors there. And many of us stop by occasionally to check out the river, especially after a rain. Or after a week of rain. Or two weeks of rain.

As the water rose, it covered a section of K-99 south of the bridge. The highway was then closed, which gave sightseers two vantage points, the old bridge and the new one, from which to view the swollen river.

When Dave and I went to see the Cottonwood, we had to park about three blocks away — a crowd had already gathered.

"Are there sharks in there?" I heard a small girl ask. "No," her mother replied.

A man picked up a rock and skipped it across the expanse of water that was covering Soden's Grove Park. Inside the park, the water reached to the zoo fence and to the ball diamond.

Dave and I continued walking south on K-99, around the curve and past the first mile road — which was completely underwater. A thin strip of K-99, the white line at the top of the curve, was dry, a pathway to nowhere. Even that little strip of dry pavement eventually ended in water.

Parents brought their kids to see the Cottonwood, just as my parents had taken me to see the flooded Arkansas River. People photographed the muddy water and the newly formed lakes which drowned the soybean fields.

We all came to see; we were there as witnesses to the flood of 2013. While looking at the out-of-bounds river, I recalled the helplessness we felt during last year's endless summer — a summer of drought and intense heat.

Last August we looked to the heavens for relief, but the sky had forgotten how to rain. It seems the sky is just not good at moderation; it may never stop raining.

*November 2009*

# GATHERING LEAVES

Thanksgiving is a time to gather the leaves: table leaves — and maybe leaves of a different sort.

My dad and my Uncle Laramie always performed the table-stretching maneuver at Grandma's house when we arrived for Thanksgiving dinner. They retrieved the leaves from the bedroom closet and pulled apart the table to make more room.

Still everyone couldn't fit, or maybe the adults just didn't enjoy our company. When we were young, my brother and cousins and I sat at the card table, where we would spill our water and giggle over inappropriate mealtime conversations.

The pre-meal wait was agonizing. I fidgeted, weakened by the savory aroma of turkey, dressing and gravy and would practically faint from hunger right there in front of the accumulating table of bounty — that we could see but not touch.

Although we grandchildren were hollow from hunger, we'd help set the table. Eventually, finally, the rolls came out of the oven. "Amen" was the sound of the starter's pistol.

Each meal was pretty much the same, the experience predictable, from the menu to the conversation.

Uncle Herman talked about government or taxes. Dad told corny jokes. Aunt Juletha found something to tease us kids about. Aunt Merle tried to convince Grandma to wear pantsuits. And Grandma asked, "Are you sure you're full?"

Many people eagerly anticipate holiday dinners, but others face them with reluctance. Some families laugh their way through the meal, telling stories and jokes. In other families there's an underlying tension; sometimes there's just too much of the same DNA in one room.

Anytime I'm at a family dinner, I like to observe the interactions; it can be instructive to observe who pushes whose buttons and why. Family gatherings can offer more head-butting than the football game on TV. And, if we care to think about it, those dynamics explain a lot about our own selves, how we became the people we are.

At any rate, these dinners are a good opportunity to learn more about family by observation — and they give us a chance to ask questions about family history.

I wish that I had asked more questions, learned the stories of my grandfather, who died when I was 6. I wish I'd had the fore-thought back then to ask Grandma more about her childhood days on the Kansas prairie in the early 1900s.

If you're curious about family history, then on Thanksgiving Day when you notice Aunt Ruth standing alone, spreading pick-les and olives on the relish tray, take a moment to ask her where Uncle Jack fought during World War II. Or maybe she'd be will-ing to share the story about how she and Jack met.

Perhaps someone could tell you more about Grandpa Fred, who once raced motorcycles, or about your Aunt Edith, who smoked cigars and was something of a card shark. Ask to hear the stories now — or forever hold your peace; as time goes on, the keepers of these stories will disappear.

If you're one of the elder family members, you could offer up your own memories and experiences. And perhaps everyone at the table, young and old, can take a turn and tell a story from his or her childhood, making it a holiday to remember.

As we look at our family tree, the branches represent people. And the leaves, well those are stories. Gather those leaves, those stories — perhaps on video or on paper, document them, write them down — before they blow away.

*The Elements*

*January 2013*

# LOVING THE WIND

"How can you call yourself a Kansan if you don't love the wind?" Dan Markowitz said in an accusatory tone when I ran into him at the Java Cat Coffeehouse.

"Um," I stammered. "Too much of a good thing?"

In a recent column, I wrote about tumbleweeds and western Kansas. While I didn't really slam the wind, neither did I fully rejoice in its existence.

"The wind, Cheryl. What's not to love?" he asked.

My friend Dan is a smart, likable guy. And he's energetic — his main form of transportation is his bicycle, which he rides year-round.

Now, I don't hate-hate the wind. In fact, I have occasionally appreciated the redemptive power of a mighty gust, one so strong that it can blow away sins. But when I don't feel a particular need for deliverance, I'd prefer to opt out of any kind of breeze over, say, 15 m.p.h.

Many Kansans do actually like the wind. Dan calls these people, including himself, "windophiles." And, if he rides his bike in the January wind without complaint, his love for gusty Kansas air must be true. So I e-mailed him later, asking him to tell me what he thinks is so great about moving air.

Growing up in Olpe in a house with no air conditioning, Dan was grateful for summer breezes that cooled the bedroom he shared with his brother.

"By the time I was a teenager, my love for the wind was deeply ingrained," he wrote. "Nothing felt better for a sweaty, dirty farm worker than a gust of fresh air on his face while baling hay in a low-lying meadow."

Dan told about one recess at St. Joseph's School in Olpe.

"A great gust of March wind caught Sister Emma just right and ripped her veil, a long, dark, heavy contraption, right off of her head. The veil sailed across the playground, leaving Sister Emma standing there, bare down to her wimple. I stifled a laugh (it was never a good idea to laugh at anything that happened in front of a nun) and set out across the playground to retrieve the tumbling veil.

"I proudly walked the veil back to Sister Emma, who expressed her appreciation for my humble service with a chocolate chip cookie from the nuns' special larder."

Dan wrote, "You asked how I like it if I'm biking into a stiff northerly breeze on a chilly January morning. The answer is, not much. You have a point. Nor do I like it in the summer when I'm riding south on Highway 99 directly into a strong hot breeze. On those days, it's particularly bad just beyond Evergreen Cemetery, where the highway starts up the hill that forms the southern edge of the Cottonwood River Valley. For some reason, the wind whooshes over that hill and blasts everything in its way like a furnace. Literally, it's taken my breath away there, leaving me unable to even curse as I huff and puff my way up to the crest of the hill, where it's hardly better."

Nevertheless, Dan says, "I think it's unfair to judge the wind by its occasional bad conduct."

I'm giving some serious thought to Dan's perspective. Wind offers benefits — such as a continual supply of fresh air. And disliking the wind only increases our annoyance. So maybe it is time to appreciate and celebrate air velocity. Wind festival, anyone?

*April 2012*

# SEND IN THE VERBS

Adjectives and nouns get a lot of use this time of year. The Kansas spring is described as everything from tranquil to tornadic.

Spring delivers dandy flowers, dangerous storms, and the sweetest days imaginable. But spring is much more than adjectives and nouns.

Rain, storm and thunder — for us, these are not just quiet little nouns; they are action-packed words. The Kansas spring is a season of verbs.

Bugs splat on the windshield. Thunder telegraphs a storm. Birds sing us awake before dawn. The sun smiles, warms our unsleeved arms. Rain washes cars, streets and cats inadvertently left outdoors.

A light wind blends aromas. In the early spring, scented trails of lilacs drift past my porch; the neighbor's spirea tickles my nose. When the honeysuckle blooms, it sweetens the night air and its fragrance slips through the bedroom window as I fall asleep.

The breeze bends young trees. Exhaling a chorus, wind sings one stanza after another; sometimes it's the longest song in the world. Wind casts no shadows, yet it breathes down our necks. Gusts pull dust from the fields and the grit scurries across the landscape.

As words of action, verbs make themselves at home in the Kansas sky. And we, below, must weather the weather, whether we like it or not.

Young and energetic, the spring sky stretches its boundaries, tests us to see how much it can get away with. And because there are no guardians of the sky, it gets away with everything. After a day of drama and destruction, the sky offers no remedy, no recourse, no reparations.

With our energy-filled atmosphere — the colliding fronts, the ever-ready wind, the moisture from the Gulf — our days and nights often rumble. The entire sky gets into the act, sets the stage for a major performance, and we're all seated in the stadium, watching, waiting, vulnerable.

During these rock-and-roll storms, we are like pioneers, exposed on the prairie, feeling small as the self-assured sky churns above us. Storms grow, taking up longitude and latitude, filling the sky with bruised clouds.

These clouds fly with impatience, turning late afternoon into darkness several hours before sunset. Lightning detonates thunder and divides a jagged sky. Each storm threatens us, a new violence as yet unmeasured. Thunder growls. It sounds like a headache feels, a persistent ache rolling across the heavens.

Sometimes I think of these storms as pirates sailing the sky. Their cloud-ships are heavy, loaded with gunpowder and cannons. I visualize the skull and crossbones flying atop each mast.

In the springtime, these pirates pillage and plunder our state. For several nights in a row they troll our skies, casing Kansas, looking for an easy mark. They pick off a town here and there, collecting gold and treasures, taking a few souls along the way.

While we're dodging hailstones or running into basements, the pirates spin the skies and slide down to earth inside of a funnel. These scoundrels take what they want, leaving behind a mosaic of disaster.

After the storm moves on, a streak of brilliant light rides the western horizon. From there, the sun slings a rainbow onto the eastern sky, an apology for its absence.

The good guys gallop in, the cavalry has arrived. They bring with them the calm evening light, and return us to a land of peaceful adjectives and nouns.

*March 2012*

# THE INTIMACY OF RAIN

Usually when spring arrives, we feel as if we've earned it.

By the time we get to March, we've had enough of dirty snow, of ice scrapers, of wind chill.

But this was a strange winter. It was disorienting to step onto the porch on a January morning and be greeted with 50-degree air. We had to ask ourselves — is it spring?

It was as if we were on a floating calendar, March-like days in December, April-ish days in February. But what really threw us off were the days we had to wear coats.

Now, I have long lobbied for a three-season year; the cold and snow, I could do without. But I never thought I would see a year that we just skipped winter.

Spring tends to be a reluctant season. Most years we have to coax spring out from behind the skirt of winter. But spring is no shy little girl this year. First she completed that hostile takeover of winter and then started tornado season in February, taking deadly aim on Harveyville.

In any given year, spring has an active to-do list: put leaves on the trees, produce blossoms, green up the grass, raise the temperature, move air from south to north, create mud, and turn the sky into a carnival of chance.

Rain is always the story of spring. A thin rain comes down like pins and needles. Dashing through a heavy rain makes us feel like we've been clobbered with a water balloon.

There's an intimacy that comes with rain. Rain touches skin, touches arms and legs; raindrops roll down our cheeks like tears. Rain becomes darkened circles on our blouses and shirts and that cold wetness adheres clothing to skin.

We connect with rain. We taste its drops, smell the earthy

fragrance as rain opens the soil. And there's just a down-home feeling that comes while listening to rain, to the steady percussion as it pelts the roof of the house.

But there are some days we don't hear the rain at all. We wake up to gray clouds and then midafternoon we glance out a window and see liquid shadows falling.

While driving through rain at night, each street lamp becomes a halo of light, a distortion of shape and color. Rain softens the edges of the world as it cleans.

And spring, of course, brings a metabolism to the atmosphere that winter lacks. The Kansas sky can fire up a good old-fashioned end-of-time thunderstorm.

Off to the west, an organ plays a hymn of thunder. The notes start out low and soft, but the tempo accelerates and the chorus crescendos with Old Testament fury. A strike of lightning, a crash of thunder and the clouds let go. We're not sure if we'll go down in flood or in flames.

Thunderstorms can be dangerous on their own, but sometimes out of the neurotic sky a certain shade of darkness emerges, a mysterious stranger, a killer tornado that headlines the next day's paper.

For a few months we will reside in this vortex of spring, the juicy season that comes with turbulence and mud and color.

OK, Miss Spring, we're glad that you're here, but how about we keep the tornadoes to a minimum this year? Just give us some sweet gentle rain, green rolling hills and a fist full of lilacs.

*August 2007*

# SEASONS IN THE SUN

"I'm drowning in a cloud of soggy air," my friend Dean complained in an e-mail.

He's not particularly fond of August.

He listed several other strikes against summer: sticky heat, annoying insects and "the garish light of a fire-filled sky."

We all loved summertime when we were kids, didn't we? At what age does the season turn against us? When did summer stop being fun?

Once upon a time, summer was the smell of chlorine, it was the shriek of the lifeguard's whistle while songs by Three Dog Night blared from the swimming pool's speakers.

Back in the days when my shorts were ratty cutoffs, summer was one good thing after another. In the small town of Pawnee Rock, it meant riding my bike five hours a day, chasing lizards at The Rock and walking a mile to the creek.

When our parents couldn't drive us to the pool in Larned, I splashed around with friends in their backyard stock tank. And now that I think about it, that was pretty much a redneck swimming pool. But, you use what you have and fun is where you make it.

Occasionally, my friends and I camped out in one of our backyards and we stayed up until 2 a.m., sneaking around town in the shadows.

Grandma took custody of us cousins for a week during the summer. We slept in hot, second-floor bedrooms in her farmhouse. The windows were wide open, but there was not a breeze within 20 miles of the place. Did it even occur to us to complain? No.

When I turned 16, some summer evenings were spent

cruising Main Street in Larned with friends. And sometimes we'd drive to Lake Wilson, where we spread our cheerful towels out on the sand, hoping for a tan but getting a burn.

Now, summers are all about SPF 45 sun block, West Nile virus, and Lyme disease. Summers mean looking for a shady parking spot so the dashboard doesn't melt. And with everyone wearing tank tops and shorts, we spot tattoos that we didn't really care to see.

I'm not a kid anymore, but I'm still a summer girl. I love the freedom that the season brings — there's no driving on ice, or wearing a coat, or being cold.

It seems as if most Kansans, bless your collective hearts, tend to favor winter over summer. Sometimes I think I'm the lone defender of summer.

While most people grumble about summer, I'm a winter grumbler. My skin is thin; it does a poor job of keeping out the cold. And if there's one thing I cannot abide in this world, it's being cold.

When people occasionally warn me about the flaming afterlife, I say, "Well, ya know, that wouldn't really be a problem for me."

Yeah, OK, summer is hot. I'll give you that. Lawns start to curl at the edges like an old newspaper. After two weeks of highs in the upper 90s, green just gives up and goes home.

August flattens the state. Highways glare as heat rises. There seems to be no buffer between us and the sun.

So, the hostilities begin. People take aim at summer; they curse the boiling thermometer with its unforgiving temperatures.

Humidity is like unwelcome houseguests that never quite get around to packing their bags.

But many people can't tolerate high temperatures and they bow to the altar of air conditioner vents. They close the drapes to shut out that "garish light of the fire-filled sky."

Summer is just not the playground it used to be.

According to my winter-loving friend, Dean, "Brightly colored beach towels lie to us all. Good times are promised but not delivered. There is no fun in the sun."

*September 2012*

# VISITING HURRICANES

Here in the Midwest, hurricanes seldom enter into the forecast, but occasionally the remnants of one will pass over Kansas and drop some rain.

Not Isaac. At a time when our land is so thirsty for precipitation, Isaac slighted us. However, we did get to see some unusual clouds that day. While the monstrous gray vortex swirled over Missouri, we noticed curved streaks of clouds to our east, the outer bands of the storm.

With Isaac nearby, I was reminded of a previous hurricane encounter.

In September 1989, my Aunt Norma and I headed to Georgia to visit my mother and stepfather, who at the time lived about 40 miles inland from Savannah. Unfortunately, Hurricane Hugo also planned to visit Savannah that week.

Hurricanes are fickle. They get stronger, they weaken, they swerve, they don't swerve; you just can't trust them. But Norma and I counted on luck and started our two-day 1,200-mile trek to visit my mom.

Hugo was headed straight for Savannah. I was a little nervous, and my aunt was a lot nervous. In 1969, Norma and Jay and their three young kids had lived on Santa Rosa Island near Pensacola, Florida, where Jay was doing his medical internship.

"The terrible part of Camille hit down the way, of course, but for a long time, even into the final night, it seemed headed straight for us," Norma recalled later. "Hurricane flags had flown for several days, radio and TV broadcast dire warnings every 15 minutes." They were evacuated.

"Water did sweep the island, two or three houses were destroyed," Norma said. "Entry onto the island was prohibited for three or four days. The damage done further west was horrible."

As we headed for the coast, Norma shared those Camille memories, making hurricanes sound very real and very frightening. Driving southeast from Atlanta on I-75, the scene was haunting. Cars moved slowly, bumper-to-bumper, headed away from the coast. Vehicles were filled with moms, dads, kids, pets and belongings.

By comparison, the southbound lanes were eerily empty. Except for us, the only other vehicles were caravans of Georgia Power trucks, the sight of which was both comforting and disconcerting.

In Kansas, tornadoes are our main threat and our evacuation route is simply down the staircase, so this trip offered me images of the fleeing-from-the-storm process.

Rather than head into the unknown, Norma and I stopped that afternoon.

"We were able to find a motel available only because Jay had a priority card with Holiday Inn," Norma recalled. "They had no openings in any of their places, but because of the priority club membership, they went to the trouble of searching out an opening for us in another motel in another town."

The storm threatened to cause serious wind damage inland, so my mom and stepdad decided that maybe they didn't want to be in the way of Hugo either. They headed inland and shared our motel room in Forsyth, Ga.

The four of us sat on the edge of the beds late that night, watching the news as Hugo approached the coast. We worried about their house and about everyone in the path of the storm. The hurricane took an 11th-hour curve to the north, making landfall near Charleston, South Carolina, as a category 4 storm.

There is no happy ending with a hurricane. More than two dozen people were killed in South Carolina and the area suffered incredible devastation. Although Hugo also caused damage in Georgia, Mom's house was fine. A can of wasp killer left on her porch railing was still standing, undisturbed. But with hurricanes, you just never know.

*September 2008*

# WAITING ON THE SKY

John Mayer has a song called "Waiting on the World to Change."

Well, I spent the first two weeks of September waiting on the sky to change. For a fortnight, we were stalked by nimbostratus clouds.

These are not your cheerful, coloring-book clouds. Nimbostratus have no sense of humor; they are dour and sullen, and apparently they had Superglued themselves to the sky. And that overcast sky rained and rained; those clouds nearly drowned us.

From one horizon to the other, the concrete sky was impenetrable. There were no corners to the clouds, no edges, no cracks into which you could wedge a crowbar to break open the blue.

There's a line in our state song, ". . . and the skies are not cloudy all day." Don't believe it.

For many days, no shadows fell upon the earth. We could only presume that the sun had been blindfolded and was being held hostage in a dark attic somewhere. I kept watching CNN for an update, but there was no report of a ransom note.

We who live on the prairie love our sky. It is as much a part of the landscape as the land itself. While the earth gives us roots and plenty of soft grass on which we can curl our bodies and fall asleep, the sky gives us flight, imagination, a place to go with our eyes, a place to go with our minds.

We Kansans love the feeling of space that the open land provides, but a great deal of that sense of freedom comes from the infinite sky that fills our days and our nights. It is the blue sky that gives us our energy, the stars that give us our passion.

When the frumpy clouds move in and unpack their suitcases, some people actually enjoy the gray days. Some thrive on the cave-like feel of dark rain.

But not everyone. I feel claustrophobic after two days of overcast skies. Clouds are my Kryptonite.

Finally — after those two long miserable weeks — when the sun finally burned through the ropes and broke free from its captors, the glistening light beamed down in a brilliant ray, kissing me on the forehead. It was like being awakened by a handsome prince.

Now don't get me wrong — I'm not a cloud-hater. I love clouds, but only the ones with ambition, only the ones that move.

Puffy cumulus, a whisper of cirrus, and even purple thunderheads — I love them all — because they come to pass. And also because they entertain me.

Clouds tumble and scamper; they evolve. They skid across the sky; they float. Wallace Stegner once called cumulus clouds "navies of flat-bottomed boats."

The sky gives us a never-ending scroll of murals — this is public art. Clouds tell us stories and urge us to invent our own.

While on a recent road trip, in the cumulus hanging over the highway I saw a bear with a book, reading to two nearby clouds, one of which looked like a boy and the other, a girl with pigtails.

It was a sweet, fairytale scene in the sky. A few minutes later, I glanced back at those same clouds. The children were gone, the bear cloud was fatter — well, you can draw your own conclusions.

When clouds collide, there is no crashing sound and you see no cumulus limping to the sideline. Clouds merge softly, yielding their territory; they reshape themselves and sail away.

And moving on is what clouds do. Usually.

But when they settle in with their gray flannel wardrobe, you may have to spend a week or two waiting on the sky to change.

*November 2011*

# NOVEMBER WIND

The wind was so strong that I expected to see a few stripes being yanked from Old Glory and watch them whip away into the atmosphere.

Stretched to its limit, a flag held onto a residential pole for dear life as raging gusts tugged at the stars and stripes.

It was a day of warm wind from the south before a day of cold wind from the north. Kansas is just a crazy, mixed-up medley of weather. I guess that's why we like it here; each day is a surprise. Some people may consider our state to be plain and ordinary, but you certainly can't say that the weather is boring; it does its best to outdo itself.

Winds that Friday clocked in at 33 mph with gusts up to 46. Certainly not the strongest winds we've ever had, but strong enough.

While we seem to always have some level of wind here, it's often just a relatively quiet stream in the background. On this particular Friday, however, the northbound 70-degree air was on a jumpin' joyride, and everything above ground was up for grabs.

In a tree-filled neighborhood, I drove through a leaf storm. My windshield was pelted with the colorful handprints of maples, oaks and Bradford pears. Just a few days earlier I had noticed how glorious the Bradford pears were in the bright sunshine. The leaves bore the colors of ripe fruit: pomegranate, mango, persimmon, pumpkin.

Even though it was mid-November, leaves still hung on many trees in town. But now wind was the victor, taking them down, dozens at a time. Dead leaves filled the gutters and I realized that in places they had formed drifts. Leaf drifts.

Huddled like old grief, jumbles of leaves found themselves stuck in the web of shrubbery, unable to move on.

The wind blasted through town. As angry as a bad boyfriend, it slammed the door on its way out, backed over the trash bins and tore off down the street.

As I drove along Fifteenth Avenue, Friday morning's trash pick-up had been completed and now the empty gray carts were lying in the street, a half-dozen of them, one after another, face down, each lid gaping in disbelief.

The arm of traffic lights reaching across Sixth Avenue swayed to the beat of the wind. Gusts sent a warm shiver up the spine of a stop sign and the red octagon shook its head back and forth, which seemed to negate its stated message.

A stout breeze may seem friendly at first, giving you a bear hug when you walk out the door, but soon you find that it's like one of those close-talking people, someone who invades your personal space, ignores social cues and never backs away.

The wind that Friday had a Southern drawl. Saturday was a different story; the wind hit us from the north. Friday, our high was near 70. The cold front on Saturday dropped the temperature to around freezing. Both days, wind was the active story.

KSN meteorologist Mark Bogner said, "With the low pressure along the strong cold front, contrasted with the fairly high pressure over the southeast, and the much stronger high pressure coming down from Canada, we get 'squeezed' in the middle, and since we don't have significant hills or trees to slow the wind down, we get lots of it here in Kansas."

Usually the wind simply blows through the margins of our lives, but some days it does a full sweep, clearing everything in its path.

One advantage to wind, however, is that we often see the American and Kansas flags as they were meant to be seen: unfurled. Here in Kansas, we definitely get our money's worth out of flags.

*December 2005*

# ODE TO WINTER

The hardwood floors are now too cold for bare feet. And mornings are no longer warm enough to sit around with wet hair.

Windshields must be scraped, but it's nearly impossible to do anything while wearing 17 layers of clothing.

Four seasons — who needs them? Really now, isn't three enough?

My friend Dean, smart though he is, actually likes cold weather. And he issued a challenge: "I think you should write an ode to winter!" he suggested in an e-mail.

"I know you're a summer gal," Dean said, "but a writer like you could find something good to say about all four seasons in Kansas."

I rolled my eyes. But later, I reread a previous e-mail — one in which he had compared these opposite seasons.

Dean had written, "The noisy summertime, with its bright and flashy colors, is like the crazy neighbor who stays up way too late — drinking beer and playing loud music all night long.

"The peaceful wintertime, with its black and white simplicity, is like a trusted friend or lover whose mere presence calms and consoles us.

"Stars shine so much brighter on a clear winter's night. Ghostly rabbit tracks remind us that we're not really alone in this mystical winter wonderland."

I can't believe it. Dean sold me on winter — with those ghostly rabbit tracks.

OK, I will write about winter —not an ode exactly, but maybe I can say a few gentle words about the season. Actually, I *do* like the silence of snow. Snow swallows sound — as if each flake absorbs a bit of noise from the world.

Sometimes flakes are heavy with moisture and the sky is as thick as milk. Other days you can follow a single snowflake to the ground where it cozies in with a pocket of friends.

As you gape at the sky, which is falling to pieces, a huge snowflake lands just below your left eye and you feel each point dissolve on warm skin.

Snow glitters in the purple glow of a street light. And night becomes a ghost town.

Winter evenings keep us indoors, where we play cards or Scrabble or Chinese checkers.

Winter is the sound of basketball shoes squeaking on the wooden court. It's the thunder of players chasing a fast break, the sudden cheer, the announcer's voice lost in the crowd. Winter is a tangle of jackets and scarves piled on the bleachers. Coat pockets spill leather gloves, which are kicked and scattered and lost for good.

When we're outdoors, we seek warmth and we are drawn to a lighted window. Winter is a church aglow at night. Candles flicker in the drafty air. Whispered prayers comfort us like a lullaby, but "Joy to the World" is the evening's benediction.

We like gathering in these large hollow buildings. We rush through doors which are hurriedly closed against the cold. We want to feel the embrace of a friend and hear the chatter of strangers because so much of winter is isolation. On these long nights, it's easy to stay at home.

The aroma of cornbread drifts through the house. Standing against the oven, we cook ham and beans and we feel safe and warm.

Now that it's winter, we will catch up on our reading. And we'll catch up on our sleep — under heavy quilts that hold us prisoner.

Eventually, winter will wear itself out. But for now, we no longer fight the darkness or the solitude. And we settle in — to the ordinary cold.

We learn to rest quietly in this ancient season.

*February 2012*

# WINTER, MAYBE

We have been slipping through winter with the greatest of ease.

Here in east-central Kansas, this has not been a snow angel kind of a year. To get angel wings fluttering on the ground we need measurable snow, and in December and January that just didn't happen. We began to think that the sky had lost its flake-making ability.

Perhaps winter simply missed a turn on its GPS or, more likely, La Niña took the jet stream for a ride. At any rate, we've lived most of the season in a warm lull, a quiet spring-like winter. The past few months, people have been wearing T-shirts, shorts and flip-flops around town.

We have had a few days of flurries, and some colder air has settled in on us again now, but for the most part, winter wintered elsewhere. Our temperatures have been freakishly mild and, as of this writing on February 9, the sky has given us only a few measly attempts at snow, light dustings of white that didn't last. That's it.

This year, so far anyway, we've escaped the white abyss, the rolling whiteouts, snow bullets that shatter when they hit our windshields.

We've had blue skies for a majority of our winter days, which is an improvement from the gray skies that so often hang around this time of year. Winter skies are usually the color of old nickels with clouds huddled together, so deep in conversation they're inseparable and even the sun can't get a ray in edgewise.

In mid-December, we did have a blast of freezing temperatures and I thought that cold air would stick around, so I wrote a column called "Winter Is Here." Then as soon as the column ran in the paper, the thermometer bounced back up to 60 degrees, making me look like a fool. You can't trust the weather in Kansas.

Or maybe, just maybe, I jinxed winter by writing that column.

Since then, we've had fabulous weather through December, January and into early February. So I decided I would write a winter-skipped-us column, and look what has happened — we fell into a cold spell. I write about the cold, it warms up. I write about the warmth, it gets cold. I can't win.

When seasons are out of whack like this, our whole ecosystem can get crazy. Snow is good for wheat and it's helpful in alleviating the drought. Freezing temperatures aid in mosquito control. With winter warmth, fruit trees and bushes start blooming early and if we get a deep frost in April, we can lose an entire crop of apples, sand hill plums and other fruits.

We've gotten off easy around here, but I've been thinking about my poor brother in Alaska. He's surely ready for spring. Alaska has kept the cold air and the snow up there this year. In January, Leon sent an e-mail with the subject line: "No gardening today" and he included a photo of the temperature reading at Fairbanks, –50, with a caption, "My coldest day ever."

OK, that kind of cold is just nuts. But there is something honest about a freezing cold day. When we're out in subzero air, we can experience some truths about who we are as individuals and as human beings. Bitter temperatures give us that man vs. nature experience, provide that feeling of being in the wilderness without us even having to leave town.

Where the seasons go from here, it's hard to guess. Winter has already been hit-and-miss with an emphasis on the miss.

February is half over and we are closing in on spring. Now we are just waiting for the dandelions.

*Departures*

*October 2006*

# 'BLESSED ASSURANCE'

A biting north wind whipped the canvas funeral tent. Unyielding clouds darkened the sky. We gathered at this hilltop cemetery to bury one of our own.

The extended family huddled for warmth under the green tent. In the brief committal service, the Mennonite pastors offered prayers and we sang "God Be with You Till We Meet Again."

Ella Schultz Dirks, my grandmother's sister and lone survivor of her generation of Pawnee Rock Mennonites, died recently at the age of 102.

She had been a widow for five years. Harvey died before they could celebrate their 75th wedding anniversary. Their son Homer passed away unexpectedly two years ago and Leon, another son, had been killed in the Korean War. A daughter, Beverly, survives.

On the morning of Ella's funeral, it was dark when I left Emporia. Light didn't reach the ground for at least an hour. The sky was heavy. Rain streaked my windshield. At the mortuary in Great Bend, I embraced my second cousin Darla. We had been grade school classmates but attended different high schools. Ella was Darla's grandmother.

Ministers Todd and Lynn Schlosser of the Pawnee Rock Bergthal Mennonite Church led the service.

"I've marveled at her strength and her resolve over these years I've known her," Rev. Todd Schlosser said. "Ella has been our eldest church member for some time."

Rev. Lynn Schlosser made frequent home visits and said, "It has been a joy to know Ella. I found a note from another pastor and she wrote, 'Ella is unfailingly cheerful.'"

"What she would do when sleep wouldn't come was to sing over and over 'Blessed Assurance' and then repeat the Lord's Prayer," she said.

"My, how she loved all of you," the pastor smiled, addressing the family. "Even at her age, Ella knew each of you individually."

"One visit stands out — the only time I spent with her that I wasn't able to get a smile. She cried and she shared how much she missed Harvey and Homer and Leon."

"Ella's song was her love for family; her story was her love for life," she said.

This was a personal eulogy. I could easily picture the minister on a home visit, tucking in a blanket around this elderly woman. And that's why we were all there — to enfold Ella Dirks with love, to gently send her on her way.

In one clear moment, I realized what I was missing for having left the fold of my hometown church. Even though I've been away for 30 years, the members know me. These people heard me wail in the church nursery, made me draw maps of Judea in Sunday School and directed me in the Sunday morning choir.

This church is made up of those with similar beliefs, but more than that, it is family. Many of us are related, descendants of the Mennonite immigrants who came to the area from Russia in 1874.

These stoic Mennonites are not the sort of people who rush at you with open arms, but they offer generous hospitality and will be at your side during a tragedy.

I saw their compassion reflected in perfect stitches on quilts that would be sold to help the needy and in the hundreds of carefully packed health kits prepared for children overseas.

Each time I return to the Bergthal Mennonite Church, there are fewer and fewer of the German faces that once filled the sanctuary. Velma is no longer there to play the organ. Her sister Glennis is gone. So too, Cleo, Olin, Ethelena, Daisy, Dan and Dauvina, Eldon and Irma, Maxlyn, Helen and many others.

These elders have gone on ahead, but they've left us their stories, they've left us their songs.

Rest well, Aunt Ella.

*April 2008*

# UNCLE JAY

When the Chihuahua left his lap, Jay brushed off the front of his robe.

"There's hair on my robe and I don't know if it's the dog's hair — or mine," he laughed.

The sunset through the windows highlighted the wispy white strands remaining on Jay's head. His short, salt-and-pepper hair was gone.

Dave and I drove to Arkansas a few weeks ago to visit my mom, Aunt Norma and Uncle Jay. Jay, at 69, was feeling pretty good when we stopped by their house that Friday evening. It had been about 17 months since the diagnosis: esophageal cancer. As a retired radiologist, he read the future on his own X-rays, but seemed to be accepting of the outcome — whatever that may be.

He told me it was a three-way contest now, between the cancer, the chemotherapy and him. The chemo was shrinking the tumors, but he was exceedingly thin and weak.

Jay's the one, the Arkansas native, who could not imagine why anyone would choose to live on the plains. He's always made fun of Kansas in a way that made me laugh. That was our game, his and mine.

One of his classic lines is about a painting of Norma's. Her painting of an old converted school bus depressed him, he said, because the surrounding emptiness reminded him of Kansas. "It looks like people went out to pick wheat, their bus broke down, and they've lost all hope."

That evening, Jay told stories as usual. With widespread flooding in Arkansas on the news, he told about the time he took his young boys canoeing on the Current River when it was swollen. He didn't realize until they were on the water how dangerous the situation was. "If one of those canoes had tipped, there's no way I could've saved any of us. The river was just too strong," he said.

As with the hundreds of other Jay stories I've leaned into over the years, I caught every word delivered in his deep voice, his Southern drawl. And with Jay, I was always prepared for a laugh; he offered plenty.

At family gatherings, he and I have naturally converged. Whenever I've felt a need to leave a room of chattering people, I've stepped outside and found Jay, smoking a cigarette.

Jay has long been one of my favorite people. He's intelligent, self-assured, a decision-maker, a family anchor.

Two years ago when my mom was in the hospital in Hot Springs, as I prepared to return to Kansas, Jay handed me $50. "Put that in your jeans," he said.

"What's that for?" I asked.

"Traveling money," he said, and changed the subject.

Jay had always taken care of me, not with cash but with his calm and steady presence. For instance, I could always relax in the backseat when he was at the wheel, knowing he could bend that Trailblazer around any curve the Arkansas Highway Department threw at him.

On that Friday night of our visit, Jay was weak but doing OK. Saturday evening, he felt miserable and was transported to the emergency room. When we left him there, he seemed to be perking up a bit.

An urgent call came from the hospital Sunday morning. As we stepped into his room, he smiled and greeted each of us by name. About an hour later, he was gone.

Life has many goodbyes. After a heartbreaking loss, we gather our wits, our resources; we carry on. And our embedded memories sustain us.

The night before Jay's memorial service, I was happy to hear laughter fill the house as we shared family memories. The master storyteller was gone, but the stories remained. As did the laughter.

Jay had taught us well.

*September 2011*

# A WELL-DRESSED MAN

The last time I saw my father, he was wearing a snappy new pair of overalls.

They were the Key brand, in the herringbone design. But Dad being Dad, at some point he had removed, most likely using his pocketknife, the diagonal stripe of green cloth on the bib which identified them as Key.

I'm guessing that Dad removed the label from the front of his overalls for the same reason he had removed the Marmie Motors nameplate from the trunk of his Chrysler. One day I noticed the tiny holes in his trunk lid and asked what that was all about. He said, "I'm not going to advertise for anyone."

Sometimes my dad would wear jeans, but most of the time he was an overall-wearing guy. During the 1990s, each April I'd meet Dad and my stepmother, Betty, at the state fairgrounds in Hutchinson for the Mennonite Central Committee Relief Sale. Betty enjoyed the quilt auction; Dad's favorite place was the general auction where tools and household items were sold.

So that's where I'd find him. Dad and I would sit on the bleachers together, silent mostly; neither of us were big talkers. We'd keep an eye on the auction and watch the people streaming past us.

It's strange now, to remember those days with Dad, 20 years ago when he was 65 and easily able to walk all over the fairgrounds, capable of confident navigation on his own. For the past five or six years his balance and his memory had both become increasingly poor. His world narrowed. At 85, he didn't get out on his own anymore.

At these MCC events, there were a number of men in overalls. As Dad and I would wind our way through a crowd, Dad would stop, make eye contact with a stranger and say, "Now, there's a well-dressed man." And the stranger wouldn't know how to take that until he realized that Dad, too, was wearing overalls. Then he gave my dad a smile and a nod.

One day, when Dad and Betty were both in their mid-60s, the three of us were in their backyard in Pawnee Rock. I don't remember how the topic came up, but Dad said, "When it's my time to go, I want to be buried in my overalls."

Betty replied, "Oh, you will not. You'll be buried in a suit." And she spoke with a certain amount of authority.

With an ornery grin, Dad protested, "But no one will recognize me if I'm not in my overalls."

Dad had, after all, worn them since he was a boy on the farm. In the earliest photos I have of him, at ages 6 and 8, he's in overalls.

As an adult, they were his work clothes of choice, perfect for a carpenter with the various loops and pockets to carry tools and nails.

About nine years ago, the herringbone version of Key overalls became hard to come by. That particular fabric was no longer made and so Dad was facing a switch to either the solid denim or the navy-and-white striped overalls.

Then I got a lead on where I might find the herringbone — at Bill's Hardware in Hartford. Theda Wolford had two pairs left in Dad's size. Dad was happy. And Betty was happy. She had been repairing his old overalls, sewing patches on top of patches. Eventually though, Dad was forced to wear overalls of the striped variety.

I learned a few years ago, and Betty was the one who mentioned it, that she and Dad had saved back a pair of those herringbone overalls for his funeral.

On a summer evening, July 29, as I stood alone beside his casket in the mortuary, I smiled through tears at my dad in his overalls. He was wearing that nice crisp pair. For some reason, I felt the urge to write a note, something to accompany him on his journey. The only paper I had on me was one of my business cards, and I wrote on the back of it, "I love you, Daddy," and slipped it into the bib pocket of his overalls, right next to his heart.

Rest in peace, my beloved father. You were a well-dressed man — and so much more.

*October 2011*

# MY FATHER'S WORLD

While going through family albums, one photo of my dad simply tackled me. I don't think I'd ever seen it before, or if I had, it didn't strike me like it did at this particular moment, two days after his death.

Standing in front of the school bus he drove, my father's arms are clasped behind him, shoulders back, chin up; he has a slight but mysterious smile. His gaze is strong and off to the distant right. My dad's unusual but confident pose brought the word "superhero" to mind.

Like most little girls, I viewed my dad as some sort of Superman. There was nothing he couldn't do. He built the house we lived in, mowed the yard, changed the oil in the car. He read to me, answered all the questions a 4-year-old girl could ask, and on Sunday mornings he put frilly white socks on my feet.

But as I grew older, I began to see that everyone has shortcomings and that some people are burdened by unresolved childhood issues.

My dad's life was difficult from day one. In 1926, he entered this world with a congenital skin condition. He was different, impossibly and visibly different. As a boy, he was ridiculed and ostracized. I can't imagine what it must have been like to live inside of his skin.

Depression sometimes took him for a ride and he had silent spells. He and my mother didn't mesh well. But as a father, he always offered gentle love and guidance.

Two days after his passing in late July, my brother and I each selected dozens of photographs to be made into a slide show for viewing at the funeral home.

Scanning the arc of Dad's life was enlightening. Although I

had known the countless things he was involved in, seeing everything at once showed me the depth and range of his 85 years on this planet.

I saw photos of him as a Lions Club member, handing out coffee to Labor Day travelers. There were pictures of him with the Cheyenne Stamp Club. My brother and I also became stamp collectors, attending Sunday afternoon meetings in Great Bend with our dad.

I found images of him mowing grass at one of the cemeteries he maintained, and a photo of him as a church officeholder. He was also Pawnee Rock's unofficial historian with a vast collection of old photographs and documents.

Dad drove a Pawnee Rock school bus for 18 years and later became the rural mail carrier, but he was a carpenter at heart and by trade. Several pictures were of him in his shop, acting as the 4-H club's woodworking leader.

He began his career with wood in the 1940s, building truck beds. Then he opened his own woodworking shop in downtown Pawnee Rock where he made sawdust for 46 years and specialized in fine cabinets and bookcases.

Betty, my stepmother, and Dad were happy together; they had 24 married years. And Dad's ornery grin was present in nearly every picture she took of him.

Photos from Betty's albums show my dad 30 feet above the back yard, cutting down a tree, limb by limb. One image has him raising, by himself, an obviously heavy metal pole for a purple martin birdhouse. Never one to ask for help, he was physically strong and fiercely independent.

Things changed. An accident at 70 made him, for the first time, temporarily dependent on others. He made a monumental comeback in less than a year. But by the time he hit 80, age and ailments began to get the upper hand.

Because these past 15 years were often focused on limitations, I was grateful that the photos reminded me of the full measure of his life.

I kept going back to that striking and confident superhero pose of Dad standing in front of his school bus. In some ways, this picture showed a father I hadn't known.

While scanning pictures that evening, I saw that Dad had put together a complete and happy life. Maybe I was just softened by emotion, but I suddenly felt as if I understood him in ways I hadn't before, in a way that perhaps only death reveals to us.

Life isn't easy. We take what we have and we make the best out of it. My dad wasn't a superhero, but he did live a life of silent courage. And his endurance and tenacity will always inspire me.

*June 2012*

# THE FIRST BUT NOT THE LAST

Father's Day is next Sunday. I've done the math, and this year I'm coming up one dad short.

But hey, that's just the way it is.

All of us have suffered a loss of some kind, and as a result we've experienced that first year when each holiday seems especially poignant.

While I was growing up, Memorial Day had its own particular meaning for my family; it was a finish line of sorts. My dad was the caretaker of the Pawnee Rock cemetery and my family spent most of each and every May preparing the graveyard for the holiday.

Dad worked hard out there; it was his way of paying tribute to the dead, and he wanted to make the cemetery a pleasant place for visitors. Dad mowed, and my mom and my brother and I trimmed grass around the stones with hand clippers. My right hand and forearm cramped after hours of squeezing those clipper handles.

When Dad stopped his mower, we'd all take a break. Finding shade under a cedar, we took turns drinking from the gallon-sized jug of water. As the day got longer, the water got warmer.

At first I thought I could honor Dad's memory at home. After all, he wasn't at the cemetery — that was just a grave and a stone. But I soon realized that I had to go to Pawnee Rock. I needed to be at the cemetery for this first Memorial Day. So Dave and I got in the car and headed west.

"I stopped to see Grandma and Grandpa," I told my dad, pressing two bouquets of plastic flowers into the soft dirt in front of his headstone. His parents are buried at the Mennonite

Memorial Cemetery several miles away.

And I told him that I remembered all of the hours he and I had worked together on these grounds, every spring, every summer, keeping it up, year after year.

My dad's grave is in the newer section, the part without any shade. The sun burned down on me and there was barely a breeze that afternoon.

Filled 10 months earlier, Dad's grave had not yet grown over with the hardy buffalo grass that knots its way across the rest of the cemetery. I sat upon that buffalo grass that had been so familiar to me as a child. Cut close to the ground, the thin, curled blades seemed like peach fuzz covering the earth.

A half-mile north of town, the graveyard was always a quiet place, but on this day the air was abnormally still. A meadowlark sang. An owl "whoo-hooed." A truck rumbled past on the county road.

Off to the east I noticed that the cedars along the fence had grown quite tall. Dad planted those trees when my brother and I were young. Dad hauled water to the cemetery in barrels and with buckets we watered each of the trees one summer, over and over.

Our history is here, Dad's and mine. After my brother went off to college, it was just Dad and me working here, in the cooler air of the mornings and the evenings.

Sitting on the grass, I reached for a handful of dirt from Dad's grave. It was dust, really, and a strong gust could lift a layer of it and scatter it with the wind. But the memories of my dad and this cemetery will never blow away; those memories are rooted in my brain just as fiercely as the buffalo grass is rooted in the Kansas soil.

*July 2008*

# WHAT WE DON'T PHOTOGRAPH

Bunny ears — most family albums have them, a picture with a boy raising two fingers behind a sister's head.

If you open a photo album of a typical Kansas family, you're likely to see birthday cakes ablaze, snapshots of kids riding bicycles and teenagers dressed for the prom.

The other day while looking through Dave's family albums, I saw pictures of a little-girl tea party, a game of lawn darts and the nuclear family (two parents, four boys, one girl) lined up on their front porch.

The Leiker albums also hold photographs from the annual family campouts.

For years, Dave's family set up tents at one Kansas lake or another. I joined the fun in the early '90s and we'd cook hamburgers, and bait hooks, and swat mosquitoes.

At the campouts, there was an annual competition. The first year I was part of the family, the challenge was to build a solar-powered coffee maker. Dave's brother, Larry, won that contest. Larry built a large, silver-colored parabola which boiled water faster than Mr. Coffee.

Another year, at Council Grove Lake, the contest was to construct the best water balloon launcher. Curt and Nancy won with a huge contraption they had hauled behind their truck. It was probably sturdy enough to launch a calf (not that we'd do that).

So the Leiker family albums are filled with photos of holidays, happy events and weekends at the lake.

What you're unlikely to find in theirs or anyone's family albums are the painful experiences. These are the things we don't photograph.

The family has been visited by one of those difficult times.

On June 22, Dave's sister, Deborah, 55, received a severe head injury in a workplace accident in Salina. She was flown to Wichita's St. Francis Hospital, where the family gathered around their unconscious daughter, sister, sister-in-law, aunt.

A tragic time like this is part of the family history. But it's not something you'd want to put in an album and return to; heart-rending events are not something we record. Nevertheless, in the hospital, I saw poignancy in so many moments: I watched Clara place her hand on Deb's arm. She leaned over, "Hi, Debbie, it's Mom. We're all here. We're all here for you."

A moving photo could have been made of Henry, as he stood behind his wife of 68 years, his hands on Clara's shoulders. There would be such tenderness shown if I had captured Dave's hand brushing Deb's hair to the side. And there was Larry with red-rimmed eyes, sitting near the bed.

These were sacred moments, the final days of a loved one's life.

Leaving the Trauma-Surgical Intensive Care Unit one afternoon, a story-telling picture could have been taken from behind as Curt and Nancy walked down the fluorescent-lit hallway, arm-in-arm, shoulders slumped in sadness.

At 4 a.m. one day, as Dave and I entered the hospital room to relieve Jim, we found him sitting beside Deb, his hand wrapped around his sister's.

"The only thing I ask," Jim said, "is that you hold her hand. I've been holding it for like 11 hours now."

During that nine-day vigil, there were many silent minutes, when no words were spoken.

These are the photographs that we don't take. Instead, we use our photo albums to recall the good times: Deb holding up a basket of fish she caught, or launching a water balloon, Deb bent over laughing.

Someday soon, we will look at the albums again. Our fingers will pause on photos of the family campouts.

Because remembering the sound of each other's laughter will always return us to our joy.

*June 2010*

# WHEN HENRY MET CLARA

From Henry Leiker's memoir: *"First I'd like to introduce my-self. I'm Henry. I'm the fifth of a family of 14. Eight girls and six boys."*

*"When I was young I had a heavy head of hair so everyone called me Harry and sometimes Wooly, clear through my school years. To go to work in 1936, I had to go through government and county records to find out for sure my name was Henry. The county records were destroyed by flood waters. Anyhow, after looking through state records for my birth certificate, I am Henry.*

*"We lived in Walker. The house we lived in burned down when Adelberg was just a baby and was thrown out the window."*

Those words reflect the unique voice of my father-in-law, Henry, Dave's dad. Henry passed away recently, having lived a full 92 years.

In 1996, he and his wife, Clara, wrote their limited-edition family memoirs, which tell the stories of their lives.

Henry wrote, *"I was walking down a Salina street one day in the spring of '40 when I noticed an attractive young girl ahead of me. She didn't seem to be in a hurry either so I caught up and asked if I could walk with her. She accepted."*

Three weeks later, Henry, 22, and Clara, 17, were married.

When Henry passed away on May 27, he and Clara were three weeks shy of celebrating their 70th wedding anniversary. But if you count the three weeks they knew each other before their wedding, they were together the full 70 years.

They made their home in Salina and raised four sons and a daughter. Henry was a flour miller by trade. He served in the U.S. Army in the Philippines during World War II. After retiring from the Salina mills, he worked as a maintenance man at a medical clinic.

In those retirement years when they were able to get out, Henry and Clara would head for the lake with their fishing poles. Family campouts were held annually at any one of the hot and windy Kansas lakes.

All the while, Henry and Clara's love held fast during both joyful years and difficult times. "He would always kiss me good-bye," Clara said the other day, "even if he was just going to the store."

Although he was a quiet man, Henry liked to make people smile so he'd tell jokes and perform magic tricks. Upon his death, it occurred to me that I had never heard this man speak one unkind word about another person. That alone seems to represent a life well lived.

Various ailments piled up on Henry, and over the last year his health failed to the point where he could no longer recover. During his final days, his family gathered around his bed — and Henry finally got to eat the cookies that his diabetes had kept at bay.

In his casket, along with a cross and a Buddy Poppy, someone had slipped a cookie into his hand. That would have made Henry chuckle.

At Salina's First Presbyterian Church, the minister offered a fine eulogy and we sang "Amazing Grace" and "Here I Am, Lord." Outside the church, the coffin was draped with an American flag.

The words of the 23rd Psalm hung in the still morning air while an honor guard from Fort Riley stood with rifles a short way from the gravesite. When the prayers ended, six soldiers fired three volleys into the air. The clear tones of "Taps" stung our eyes as the bugle sent the word of mourning across the land.

Those six soldiers then lifted the flag from the coffin and in regimented unison stepped to the side, where they folded Old Glory with deliberate respect.

With white-gloved hands, the staff sergeant presented the flag to Clara "on behalf of a grateful nation."

Rest in peace, Henry.

*July 2013*

# SALUTING A LIFE

"Whoop — whoop — whoop!" A Salina police officer hit his siren to clear an intersection as the funeral procession began.

"They're doing those 'whoops' for your mom," I told Dave as we drove away from the church. Headed toward the cemetery, several police officers played leapfrog in the inside lane. One officer held open an intersection until his replacement arrived, then he zipped ahead to the next stoplight.

At the cemetery's entrance, next to his car in the roadway, a policeman stood at attention, holding a salute until the last car turned. Each of the five funerals I've attended in Salina have been graced with a police escort. And with each final salute, my eyes have filled with tears. It's a gesture of respect for the life that has passed.

My mother-in-law, Clara, lived 90 years, a long and full life. She shared 70 of those years with her late husband, Henry.

During the visitation, one of Clara's neighbors said to Dave with total sincerity, "I just loved her."

Dave replied, "Her strength of character stayed with her until the very last minute. If she could speak at all, she'd say 'thank you' to the hospice nurses. That was just her way."

I knew Clara to be a kind soul. She had a good heart and she accepted all of us, her family and others, exactly as we were.

More than anything, Clara loved family gatherings. She and Henry had some health issues when we held the annual family campouts 20 years ago, but they camped in tents like the rest of us. Clara was the first one out with a fishing pole in the morning and the last to pull in her line at night.

Like many mothers, anytime we left her house Clara gave us something to take home: sandwiches or cookies. Last Thanksgiving as we backed out of her driveway, Clara stood at the front door, her posture uncertain with pain and age, and waved good-bye. "Mom waving — that's the image I'll always remember of her," Dave said.

As her health declined this past year, her sons spent time with her on weekends, taking her out for meals and errands. Clara stayed in her home through Christmas, then she moved in with her son, Curt, and his family near Manhattan.

Eventually she needed constant medical care and spent the last couple of months in medical facilities. Dying isn't easy; there's often pain and suffering. The hospice made Clara as comfortable as possible, offering her strawberry ice cream and morphine.

As bystanders, we observe a loved one's physical abilities diminish and watch the tapestry of life unravel before us. We think of how much this person has meant to us, how she has enriched our lives. We also can't help but think of our own mortality, so we pull our own tapestry a little bit tighter around us.

Ninety years can go by like a moment in time. At her bedside we felt that power of time rush past us. What matters most in this world is the love we give, and Clara had a giving heart.

It is love that connects us. Our family appreciated the kindnesses: memorial gifts, cards and words of sympathy, the police escort. Clara's church provided a meal for the family after the burial. There was food left over, and just as Clara would have done, the ladies of the church sent us all home with sandwiches and grapes and cookies.

# Being a Kid

*December 2013*

# MAJOR ASTRO

On schoolday afternoons from 1962 to 1973, *Major Astro* aired on a Wichita TV station.

As Major Astro, Tom Leahy Jr. wore a white space suit and sometimes held a helmet in the crook of his arm. Leahy hosted a cartoon program and pretended to broadcast from a space station orbiting Earth. Later, his show was supposedly beamed to us from the moon and points beyond.

We kids in central and western Kansas were lucky to have Major Astro. In between cartoons, he talked about rockets and the solar system, and he led thousands of kids gently into the Space Age.

These were thrilling times. In 1957, when Russia successfully launched a satellite, Sputnik, the Space Race was on. Tainted with Cold War threats and fears, the race wasn't a friendly competition. Feeling the pressure, U.S. schools began to emphasize science and math.

On May 25, 1961, President Kennedy challenged the country: "I believe that this nation should commit itself to achieving the goal, before this decade is out, of landing a man on the Moon and returning him safely to the Earth."

July 1969: mission accomplished.

I've been thinking about Major Astro after hearing recent news that Tom Leahy's widow, Wilma, had donated memorabilia from the TV program to the Kansas State Historical Society. Leahy died in 2010 at age 87.

Major Astro was a hero to Kansas children, an icon. If you mention the name to anyone who grew up in the western two-thirds of the state during the '60s and early '70s, you'll likely have an instant bond. "Major Astro" is shorthand for "Hey, remember when you were a kid?"

After school, my brother, Leon, and I scooted down to the basement to watch *Major Astro* on our black-and-white 13-inch TV, which pulled in the signal through an antenna at the side of our house.

"I won a set of 10 ride tickets at the state fair one September," Leon remembered. "I had sent in a postcard with the three space words and he drew it from his squirrel cage on the air. The tickets came just in time, on the Saturday morning before we left for Hutch. You and I split them."

I was watching with Leon when Major Astro pulled my brother's postcard from the hopper. I don't know which was more exciting, Leon winning the tickets, or having Leon's existence recognized by Major Astro — on television!

"The family went to Hutch on another weekend to see Major Astro arrive in a red helicopter for the opening of a department or furniture store," Leon said. "We stood in the parking lot, and he landed in a vacant lot near us. It was the first time I had seen a helicopter fly in real life."

When I mentioned Major Astro on Facebook the other day, my cousin Laramie Unruh, who lives near Wichita, posted his prized autographed photo of Major Astro.

Laramie wrote, "Shortly before he passed, my family and I were at a local restaurant and we saw Mr. Leahy come in with his family. As we left, I went over to their table and I told him, 'Some people still think it is pretty exciting to see Major Astro.' His kind smile showed his appreciation."

The Space Age was a fascinating era, and Major Astro put interplanetary travel into a language kids could understand, making it easier for us to dream big. Every day he projected us all into outer space, signing off with "Happy orbits, boys and girls."

*February 2010*

# GRANDMA'S GHOST CHAMBER

Last week, on a cold winter's night when the wind was scaring up noise outside, I pulled the blankets to my chin. At that moment, Grandma Unruh came to mind.

When my brother and cousins and I spent nights with her during the winter, Grandma would come upstairs to check on us. At breakfast she'd always report, "You looked cold, so I put another quilt on you girls in the middle of the night."

With six quilts fastening us to the bed, we couldn't roll over, but at least we were warm.

Grandma's place, a mile or so northwest of Pawnee Rock, was like many Kansas farms. The two-story home was sheltered on the north by cedars. The farm had a handful of outbuildings and the place was guarded by a watchdog named Shep.

The upstairs was unheated in the winter, without air conditioning in the summer, and a little bit creepy all year round. As we climbed the enclosed staircase, drafty air swirled about us, as if we were being hugged by ghosts.

Haunted? Probably not. I'm pretty sure the creepiness we felt was something we brought upon ourselves.

I'll bet you had childhood sleepovers at which you did your best to frighten yourselves, succeeded and then spent the night deciphering the sounds of monsters.

We grandkids spent many nights at Grandma's house. And I considered my cousin, Mary, to be worldly and wise because she was six years older than me and from the big city of Great Bend.

During her junior high and high school years, Mary often brought along a friend. Mary, her friend and I would sleep in the bedroom that had belonged to Mary's mom. My brother, Leon, slept down the hall in Uncle Laramie's room. And Brenda,

Mary's little sister, a few years younger than me, got stuck sleeping with Grandma.

In those years before *The Texas Chain Saw Massacre* (1974), Mary and her friend regaled us with urban legends of the day which seemed to always be about a young couple parked out in the country and that couple encountered a human who, unfortunately, had met with some form of evil in the woods and had a missing arm, leg or head.

Since I didn't have access to fresh horror stories myself, when it came time for my turn at storytelling, I often relied on the classic "Golden Arm" tale.

We were in the perfect theatre for ghost stories, the upstairs of that old farmhouse. On winter nights, the window panes, loose in their frames, would rattle in the wind. During spring and summer, violent thunderstorms shook both the house and our nerves.

As a town kid growing up surrounded by occupied homes, I felt vulnerable on the farm at night. A lone house seemed like a lightning rod for storms and for trouble.

We were about ten miles from Larned State Hospital, where the criminally insane were housed. Once, during a high school basketball game, the principal announced over the loudspeaker that a patient had just escaped from Larned State Hospital. He warned everyone, "Before you get in your cars tonight, be sure to check the back seat."

At Grandma's house, the city lights of Larned were a visual backdrop to the southwest, and the threat of an escapee looking for food, shelter or victims seemed very real.

Inevitably, as we told our ghost stories, Shep would start barking at the edge of the dark field. When Shep's barking suddenly quit, we stopped breathing. Was she silenced? Our imaginations would fly like the wind.

I reasoned, as any 9-year-old might, that if Shep were disabled, all we had standing between us kids and the bad guy was my pacifist Mennonite grandmother and Grandpa's shotgun, which she kept behind the dining room door.

But, on a previous occasion, I had watched Grandma wring the neck of one of her chickens to make us lunch. So during those wide-eyed moments in the night, I felt oddly comforted by

Grandma's seeming enjoyment of killing chickens.

Between the two of them, Shep and Grandma managed to keep us safe from storms and from intruders.

Like any other set of kids who tell stories in the dark, we would scare ourselves silly, realizing too late that we'd gone too far. But then, the next time we stayed at Grandma's house, we'd tell those stories all over again.

*June 2008*

# THE CARPENTER

The saw's teeth kept getting caught in the wood.

"Pull your arm straight back," my dad told me.

The board wobbled; 40 pounds of girl wasn't enough to hold the piece of wood in place. Determination couldn't overcome a lack of muscle and weight. It was easy, of course, when Dad stood behind me, his left hand holding the board steady and his right hand on mine, guiding the saw.

He showed me how to start the cut by pulling the saw backward, toward me, slicing the edge first, following the straight pencil line I had drawn on the wood. He explained that a person has better control over the blade when pulling than pushing it.

My dad was a carpenter. When he graduated from high school in the mid-1940s, he built wooden truck beds for a business in Pawnee Rock. A few years later he opened his own shop and became a cabinet maker, doing custom woodworking for others.

He had a woodshop on Pawnee Rock's Main Street. This red brick building offered a large work space. Plate glass windows looked out toward the north and the west.

As a youngster, I spent a lot of time in his shop. I was often in Dad's charge, which probably decreased his productivity level by about 50 percent.

While my mom was working and my brother was learning his addition facts, I hung out with Dad, inhaling the odor of turpentine and freshly cut sawdust.

Dad let me build things myself. I could use anything from his box of scrap lumber. I'd grab a saw or a hammer and nails and have at it.

When I wasn't creating some odd thing, I watched Dad. On a

bookcase he was building, he'd use a nail set and drive nails below the wood's surface. He'd cover those holes with wood putty then sand them down.

Sanding was always on the agenda. Sometimes he used the electric sander, sometimes a sanding block, progressing from coarse paper to a fine grade. When he was done, the wood felt as smooth as the inside of my arm.

Work for him was in the details, making things look nice, meeting his own high expectations for each job. And if something didn't go right, he'd say, "Oh, fiddlesticks."

My dad was the woodworking project leader for 4-H and when I was a teenager I built a cedar chest. The county fair was in August, so the work was done in the heat of the summer.

I sanded that thing silly. On the largest pieces of cedar, I stirred up dust with the electric sander. On the small pieces I sat outside his shop in the shade using a block of wood wrapped in a piece of sandpaper.

Once the chest was put together, it was time for the finish. At dawn I'd walk the two blocks to Dad's shop (he was already there) and I'd add a coat of varnish before the day's heat turned the varnish to a mess of goo. Each evening, I'd go back to the shop and sand the chest again with fine paper, preparing it for the next coat of varnish.

Surely I was something of a pest, a girl who asked a hundred questions a day, but never did I get the impression that I was in the way.

In his shop, my dad showed me how to hammer a nail and how to saw a board. But the most important thing he showed me was that I mattered.

*March 2006*

# GRAVEDIGGER'S DAUGHTER

Whooff! The first chunk of sod skidded across a piece of plywood.

My dad sliced the ground again with his spade, tossing another grassy clump onto the plywood sheet which, by day's end, would be covered with a mound of loose dirt.

For many years, my father took care of the Pawnee Rock Township Cemetery. As a little girl in the '60s, I climbed trees and played among the tombstones as if the cemetery were my own front yard.

And when Dad dug graves, I was nearby. I sat on flat stones, studied the glinting mica in the granite and dissected slim blades of buffalo grass.

During his rest breaks, I lowered myself into the damp hole. Coolness seeped from the scarred walls, which had scoop patterns and dangling cedar roots. I rubbed my fingers over the earth where it had been made shiny by the back of the shovel.

With no day care or preschool in Pawnee Rock, for my dad it was often take-your-daughter-to-work day.

I've recalled those childhood moments lately because my father has a birthday on Sunday. It's a big one — he turns 80.

This sounds odd I know, but many of my favorite Dad memories come from hanging out with him at the cemetery.

In a small town, folks take on whatever jobs are available and do the work that needs to be done.

Carpentry was my dad's primary occupation, but also for 18 years he drove a school bus. He was a substitute rural carrier and later delivered mail full-time. And he was the caretaker of three area cemeteries.

The Pawnee Rock cemetery is a half-mile north of town.

On this quiet hill is where bodies go to their eternal rest, where meadowlarks sing and bull snakes slip through the knotted grass. Under summer skies, hawks ride on the air currents and south winds wail through the cedar trees.

Morticians called our house with news of a death and Dad usually had two days, maybe three, to open a grave, regardless of the weather. He had a couple of guys he could ask to help out. Only on rare occasions did he make a call to LaCrosse for a backhoe operator to dig a grave. He didn't want the ruts that the backhoe made. And besides, for Germans like us, it's just easier to do things the hard way.

"Once it took us all day just to get below the frost line," I remember Dad telling me about digging in the winter.

In the summer, grave-digging started before sunrise and stopped at midmorning. After supper, Dad picked up the shovel again and worked until lightning bugs flickered.

Before he ever cut the ground, Dad laid down a sheet of plywood to catch the loose dirt. This kept the nearby grass clean and nice-looking afterward. Then Dad screwed together a wooden frame, which created an outline for the grave. Once the initial rectangle was cut into the soil, he made sure to dig the walls straight down.

As I grew older, I sometimes helped Dad dig and I also filled in graves after the burial. Pushing dirt into a hole was much easier than extracting it.

Opening and closing graves was just part of the cemetery work. My regular job was to trim grass around stones while Dad mowed. He and I could tell you the location of every family plot in that graveyard — every Schmidt and Dirks and Unruh.

My dad and I spent many days together in that old cemetery. These memories will live as long as I do. When it's my turn to blow out 80 candles, I'll still recall working alongside my father.

Thanks, Dad. Happy birthday.

*December 2010*

# AUNT CORA

My Great Aunt Cora had not crossed my mind for some time. Then last week I ran across a book she gave to me when I was maybe 9 or 10.

While I've always appreciated the gift, I've also always wondered what possessed her to give a child Norman Vincent Peale's *The Power of Positive Thinking*.

I don't know whether I looked like a melancholy kid or whether she just wanted to pass on a book that had meant a lot to her. Since I was a fairly happy youngster, I assume it was the latter.

Now I didn't know Aunt Cora well at all. On my family's annual visits to Arkansas to spend time with my maternal grandparents, we'd drive around Fayetteville to visit my great aunts and uncles.

Aunt Cora was a retired teacher and she could still throw a look, so my brother and I did what was expected of us — we sat quietly on uncomfortable furniture for 45 minutes while the adults talked about people we didn't know.

After several years of these annual visits, my brother and I were surprised when one day Aunt Cora brought out a basket of toys for us to play with. The next year, she told us that we could each take two toys home with us. I selected tiny plastic animals — a pink elephant, and a squirrel with a retractable tape measure attached to the nut in its mouth.

It was the following year that Aunt Cora said something like, "I want you to have this," as she handed me *The Power of Positive Thinking*. Her signature was inside the cover and sections of the book had been underlined.

The next time I saw Aunt Cora, she was in a nursing home,

and she never recovered from the stroke.

*The Power of Positive Thinking*, published in 1952, was my first introduction to the power of thought, a topic that continues to fascinate me, and so I've always been grateful for the gift.

Last week as I looked over passages that Aunt Cora had underlined in the book, I pondered her early life in Sheridan County, Kansas. I checked family records and did the math. Cora was 15 when her (and my grandfather's) mother died in 1907. She was the second-eldest child and the eldest girl.

Two months after Cora's mother passed away, her 3-month-old brother died. After the mother's death, some of the kids were taken in by other families. I've heard that it was largely because of Cora's efforts that the siblings stayed connected and that they later got into the normal school, now Fort Hays State University, and became teachers.

She taught school, was married at age 50, and became a widow less than four years later. Cora was the family matriarch and could be rather demanding. Perhaps that strong personality came from taking charge of her siblings at age 15.

While I'll never know most of Aunt Cora's stories, memories of her are refreshed each time I see the book. The passages she underlined make me curious about her vulnerable side.

During this season of giving, I'm thinking about this book that Aunt Cora gave me.

Now, we're not always able to put deep personal meaning into everything we wrap, but maybe this year, it would be fun to select one person and give him or her an item that we treasure, and to share the significance of the object with the recipient.

Gifts from the heart are the ones that are cherished.

*May 2012*

# LEADING BY EXAMPLE

This week we celebrate mothers. When you think of your own mother, what's the first image that comes to mind? Each of us could tell a different story.

For me, I see my mom standing in front of a bookshelf, in a bookstore or maybe a library, several books already in the crook of her arm. Her head is tilted to the right as she reads titles on the vertical spines.

Both Mom and Dad read to my brother, Leon, and me when we were young, but it was Mom who was the primary word-gatherer and word-peddler in our family.

She subscribed to newspapers from Hutchinson, Larned and Great Bend. *Newsweek* and other magazines came in the mail, and we made weekly trips to the Cummins Memorial Library in Larned.

We probably weren't the typical family when we sat down at the dinner table. When Mom yelled "Supper's ready," that was a signal for the rest of us to grab our reading materials and head for the kitchen.

Don't worry; there was conversation as well. "Pass the potatoes, please." And, "Could I have some butter?"

Our kitchen had a built-in table; three sides were open and the fourth side was attached to the wall. I sat on one end of the table reading a comic book or science fiction. Leon, on the other end, likely had either a *Mad* magazine or a political science book. Dad leaned a folded newspaper against the wall to read. My mother had a magazine in her lap.

It's not like we avoided conversations. After school, I chattered endlessly to Mom. And I spent a lot of time hanging out with my dad, too. My brother and I played in the yard:

baseball, soccer and football, and we also had the occasional fight. So there was plenty of interaction. Suppertime was peaceful and quiet; it was reading time.

When Leon and I were in grade school, Mom bought a brand new set of encyclopedias. I'm not sure how these books were acquired — maybe they were purchased weekly from a grocery store, or maybe one lucky day the shadow of an encyclopedia salesman fell across our porch.

Anyway, Compton's Encyclopedia was the centerpiece of our living room bookshelves, a world's worth of knowledge in one set of books. I'd select a volume and sit on the couch with my reading for the day. I learned about U.S. presidents and studied the parts of a flower. In the section on the human body, plastic overlays showed the skeletal and circulatory systems and the organs. I was fascinated.

Even though our family didn't have a lot of money, Mom wanted to give us kids what we needed for a good education. She always felt deprived because she had wanted to go to college but felt that her parents didn't have the money to send her.

She never gave up, though. Mom earned her degree, one class at a time. She started college in the mid-'60s, when Barton County Community College opened, and graduated from Wichita State University in 1982 with a degree in social work.

While my brother and I could've gone in any direction, we both spend our days working with words. Leon was a journalist for more than 30 years, and a textbook copyeditor on the side. Now he edits and produces books in and about the Alaska Native languages. And me, well, I just love putting words together; I can't imagine doing anything else.

Mom never insisted that we read, but she made it seem so inviting. She led, and we read, by example.

*October 2012*

# LIBRARY LOVE

When I was a little kid, the best thing about my hometown library was, well, that it had books. But the second best thing about it was that it was right next door to our house.

Our property was adjacent to the fire station. The red brick fire station also housed the city hall. It was inside the city hall that the library came into existence.

Memories of that old Pawnee Rock library came to mind last month when I gave a book talk at the Gridley Branch of the Coffey County Library. Gridley librarian Janet Birk and other residents who showed up for the event gave me the small-town welcome and made me feel right at home.

When I first stepped into Gridley's library, my thought was that if I had had a library as nice as this one when I was a kid, I would've kept a sleeping bag stashed in a corner of that building, because that would've been my home away from home.

In the 1990s, Coffey County invested in its people wisely; it built libraries. And the county seat of Burlington was not the only one built; new library buildings were constructed in the outlying communities of Waverly, Gridley, Lebo, LeRoy and New Strawn.

For a Kansas town of 250 residents, Gridley has a fabulous resource with the library, which has 4,186 square feet. Compare that to the Pawnee Rock Library of my childhood which had, I don't know, maybe 120 square feet if you count the empty space between the two sets of bookshelves and the table where the librarian sat.

OK, it's totally unfair to compare the libraries of these two small towns because times have changed so much since the mid- to late '60s. And the thing was, I loved our little Pawnee Rock

Library. At that point, I didn't know to compare. I was delighted to have what we had.

Pawnee Rock's library was operated by volunteers and was only open one or two days a week. I didn't have to go far to get there, of course; I just had to walk past the two huge garage doors (labeled Fire Dept. No. 1 and Fire Dept. No. 2) where the fire engines were kept. At least one window on the first garage door was always broken out and the smell of rubber tires and cold cement hung in the air as I walked past.

Inside the library, the décor was rather stark. OK, there was no décor. There were just several tables and folding chairs for the city commission meetings. Next to the filing cabinet in the back of the room was a doorway which opened to a one-cell jail.

The floor was gray concrete and the bookcases stood in the front corner of the room near the door. The library had perhaps 200 books in the permanent collection, and maybe 60 to 80 rotating books that were changed out twice a month by the Central Kansas Library System.

Our library wasn't much by today's standards, but back then we didn't expect so much. We were simply happy to have what we had. And now, as an adult, I'm grateful to those in the Pawnee Rock community who made the library happen.

But, yeah, I would have been crazy about a library like Gridley's. If we'd have had that in Pawnee Rock, I surely would have rolled out my sleeping bag on the carpeted floor and drifted off to sleep inhaling the fragrance of books.

*October 2005*

# TOYS IN THE ATTIC

One of my favorite childhood trinkets was a tiny light bulb which was not much bigger than a multi-vitamin tablet.

Every night I would stand on my bed and hold the bulb up to the overhead light for a minute. Then, in the dark, it emitted an eerie purple glow. When the light faded, I tucked the bulb under my pillow for the night. It was a comfort toy.

But this treasure disappeared many years ago. I outgrew the bulb and it got misplaced. Since it was a favorite object, I've described it to Dave. On visits to antique stores, we've kept our eyes open for a similar bulb, but have never found one.

Some pieces of childhood are gone forever. And, that's OK. Growing up is a process of releasing things, of letting go.

However, I did find many other toys on a recent trip to my family home. The house and many belongings will be auctioned soon.

Years ago, Dad stashed our toys in the attic. I had never been up there. Because the attic's entryway is directly above the stairwell, access is somewhat treacherous. Dad always used 2 X 8s as a scaffold, balancing a stepladder on those boards.

Dave found a way up that seemed less suicidal and he climbed into the attic to retrieve long-forgotten items. I climbed the ladder myself and peeked into the attic for the first time.

Dave hauled down boxes as well as a doll bassinet that my dad had made for me. It didn't get much use because I was more of a tomboy than a girly girl.

As I pawed through the items, my childhood passed before my eyes. I pulled out piece after piece of my youth: tiny books, a few cloth dolls, a cloth turtle and even a sock monkey. I found Lego bricks, Lincoln Logs, Tinker Toys. There were wooden blocks and tiny green Army men. I had forgotten about the plastic horseshoes and my brother's helicopter.

And I ran across my brother Leon's kid-sized leather football helmet and shoulder pads, his model aircraft carrier, and my "Deputy" cap gun with the white plastic grips.

I imagine most of us experience warm feelings when we find mementoes from our youth. Picking up these treasures, we find that the energy of our childhood still vibrates in them.

The cap gun wasn't my favorite toy, but even it pulled me back to the days when I was a platinum-haired, 5-year-old girl.

Tops! I found the metal toy tops my brother and I played with. And Leon's gyroscope.

In the attic were lots of metal toys: dump trucks and tractors, a combine and other farm implements, tiny cars and a transport trailer.

All of this metal! A kid could get hurt playing with toys that have sharp edges. I don't know how we survived.

In a box of odds and ends, I found flash cards that Leon and I had made out of cereal boxes. Using black crayons, we wrote multiplication and division facts on rectangular pieces of cardboard. I tossed a lot of junk and salvaged a couple dozen items.

And I picked through one box until the only things remaining were random jigsaw puzzle pieces. I dumped those in a trash bag so I could reuse the box. An old newspaper lined the cardboard box.

And there I saw it, caught in the fold of the paper. The same color as the yellowed newsprint was my tiny, glow-in-the-dark light bulb.

And it still works. After exposure to a light source, the bulb puts out the same weak purple glow.

This little light of mine is finally back where it belongs: under my pillow.

*December 2011*

# ONE KOLACHE TOO MANY

If you're not over-consuming calories this month, then you're just not trying. Sugar, butter and chocolate are all over December like needles on a Christmas tree.

Holiday sweets may exist even in your memories. If you're like me, you maintain a dessert folder in your brain.

This time of year I always open that folder and recall Christmas stollen, a German bread-like fruitcake. One year, maybe it was 1992, some friends gave Dave and me a loaf of this holiday bread with its candied fruits, nuts, raisins and spices. The stollen tasted so good that even after two decades, I haul out that memory every December.

I'm not much of a baker and won't actually make it, but I did look at the stollen recipe in *Prairie Meals and Memories*, by Carolyn Hall. Her book offers recipes and tells stories about her childhood in the rural community of Olmitz, located in Barton County.

Hall writes that her father was frustrated because her mother could never make Christmas stollen exactly the way his mother did. But perhaps his wife simply could not compete with a memory.

Also in Hall's book, I came across her recipe for the German pastry, kuchen. Although the preparation is somewhat different, Hall notes that the ingredients are the same as for kolache, a Czech pastry.

Now this is where I always run off the track: kolaches. It's silly, I suppose, but even after 30-some years, whenever I think of kolaches, my faces flushes with shame.

When I was about 15, I babysat for a family across the street. The father, Ray, was a psychologist at Larned State Hospital.

They were nice people. His wife, Becky, treated me like a friend and we got along well.

One evening I was called over to babysit. Before they left, Ray proudly showed me his baking project; he had made kolaches. There were five on a large plate. As they left for the evening he said, "Help yourself. And let me know what you think."

They were large round pastries, with a couple of tablespoons of fruit filling in the center. After they left, sure, I tried one. It had apricot filling and it was so good. My taste buds were satisfied but yet I wanted to give the baker my full support and encouragement, so I had another. It had poppy seed filling and I spit that out into a napkin and threw it in the trash can.

When they came home, Ray looked at the serving plate and saw two empty spaces.

"You had two?" he gasped. "It took so long to make them." I thought he was going to cry.

Well, I was just a kid and had misread the situation. My grandmother measured her baking ability by whether or not we took seconds.

I felt bad and since then I have cringed every time kolaches came to mind. Trying to do the right thing sometimes ends up being the wrong thing. I felt like I had stolen the joy from him and I've carried that uncomfortable feeling for decades.

Maybe Ray, wherever he is now, remembers the incident too, but probably it's been long forgotten. In any case, it's time for me to let it go and enjoy kolaches without the guilt.

Yeah, it's ridiculous to have carried that moment as a bad memory for so many years. And Christmas, the season of joy, is a good time to let it go.

I'm sure we all hold onto useless scraps of darkness, of guilt or shame. When we release the unpleasantness from our memories, we are able to shine more brightly. And, we are free to eat more kolaches.

*March 2011*

# THE WESTERN FLYER

My mom once told me, "After we gave you that bike for your birthday, we never saw you again."

That's true. I was on that bike like a birthmark. I rode it around Pawnee Rock on summer days from morning till night. I knew every bump on every sidewalk in town. Our dog, Patches, a rat terrier, followed me everywhere I went.

But then, who doesn't like riding a bike? My guess is that each one of you can still describe your own childhood bicycle.

One April Saturday just before my sixth birthday, Mom took my brother and me to Great Bend to purchase a bicycle. Up until then, I had been riding a scraped and dented 16-inch bike that had been passed around from kid to kid to kid.

Because many of our toys were secondhand, I hadn't expected a brand new bike, but here we were in Western Auto, inhaling the fragrance of new tires. The center aisle of the store was a tangle of closely placed bicycles, each one depending on its kickstand, chrome handlebars shining like mirrors.

When I saw the bike with sparkling green-blue metallic paint and platinum-colored fenders, I knew it was the one. This 24-inch bike was the perfect size and I loved the brand name: Western Flyer.

A few days later, my dad drove his pickup to Great Bend and hauled home a boxed version of the bike. That evening, in between jumps up and down, I handed Dad wrenches as he put my bike together. I skipped supper that night, riding my brand new bicycle into the sunset.

I soon became handy with wrenches myself, using them to raise the seat or to remove tires. My brother taught me how to patch an inner tube. Flat tires were common — along sidewalks and the edges of the dirt streets were goathead thorns, also known as puncture vines.

I wanted to be out in the community, to see activity, movement and life. I rode to the frayed edges of town, kept track of who was building a garage, who was painting their house, which kids got yelled at by their mothers. I knew where everyone lived and what everyone was doing. Had there been a call for a private eye or a town spy, I could've done the job.

My friend Amy and I found the schoolyard to be a great place to ride since the entire playground was covered with asphalt. (Dangerous for children, yes, but on the bright side, no mud!) We rode our bikes slalom-style through the swings.

Sailing down the hill near Pawnee Rock State Park was as close to flying as a kid could get. We just had to stay out of the way of the salt plant trucks which were also flying down the hill, headed for the depot.

My bicycle allowed me to be a visible and moving part of the community. I imagine my bike and my dog and I were something of a fixture in town just like Willard the welder and Bruce the old man who stood on street corners.

No possession gave me as much joy as that bicycle. Each pedal stretch energized me, I took in fresh air, I raced the wind.

Times have changed, and these days I realize just how lucky I was to be able to have that freedom, the trust of my parents and the safety that my small hometown offered. It was a pretty good life for a girl and her dog and her bike.

*October 2008*

# MY SOAPS

In the store the other day, I stood before an array of bath soap. Blue packages, green ones, yellow ones, white. Which brand to choose?

There's Irish Spring — which I don't buy because its scent is overwhelming and because 20 years ago its television commercials annoyed me.

But now, as I try to recall the Irish Spring tune, my mind drifts instead to Lucky Charms commercials. All I can come up with is "they're magically delicious," which is obviously wrong for Irish Spring.

Standing in the soap aisle, I look for something without a strong fragrance. Aromatherapy is an overused marketing concept and to tell you the truth, my nose is a little tired of smelling perfumes all day long.

Nearly every household product is scented: dish soap, lotions, shampoos and cleaning products, including bleach. I think it's inappropriate to make bleach smell pleasant — should a person really be sniffing that stuff?

Remember the smell of . . . nothing? Remember what air, fresh air, used to smell like? I want some of that.

OK, I'm stepping down from my aromatic soapbox now.

Ivory does have a scent, but not an overpowering one, so I selected a three-pack of the white bar soap which has been around forever (or at least since 1879).

When I was a kid, there were fewer soaps to choose from and Ivory was the brand my mother purchased.

My mom kept a bar of Ivory at the bathtub (Ivory floats!) and one at the sink. My dad used Lava soap, the gritty green bar that was good for scrubbing paint and grease off hands.

It's been years, I suppose, since my last Ivory purchase. As I unwrapped a fresh bar, the clean scent reminded me of a dog, a dog that I carved out of a bar of soap when I was a kid.

When my brother and I were 10 and 8, respectively, a woman from our Mennonite church, Ruth Deckert, gave art lessons to Leon and me. At her kitchen table, Ruth taught us how to draw. We used soft-leaded pencils and gummy art erasers. Then we progressed to charcoal and pastels. At some point, Ruth asked us to each bring a bar of Ivory soap; we were going to carve an object.

I think my brother made a fish. And I carved a dog, or at least the head and shoulders of something that looked sort of like a Labrador retriever, a white Lab obviously.

The soft fragrance of Ivory settled into the folds of my brain as I nicked away at the soap, transforming the rectangular bar into a lopsided dog bust with one ear sort of misplaced.

Ruth wrapped up the white Ivory bits from her kitchen table, the pieces of soap that were neither dog nor fish and said, "Give these shavings to your mother and she can put them in with her next load of laundry."

I think I threw the soap scraps away.

That soap dog with the misplaced ear became a gift to my grandmother in Arkansas. I'm grateful that she didn't use it herself as soap — so easily it could've gone the way of soap-on-a-leash, but Grandma, bless her heart, placed my Ivory dog on her living room bookshelf.

Each time I visited my grandparents I'd pick up that white Labrador retriever off the shelf and admire my first piece of sculpture. And I'd bring it to my nose for a long inhalation.

That work of art has been lost to time, but now that I'm using Ivory these days in the shower, the soapy-dog smell comes back each time I lather up. And as dogs go, the Ivory soap ones smell pretty clean.

*May 2005*

# THE OLD FAYETTEVILLE PLACE

I hang onto books, especially my favorite ones.

As a youngster I must have read *Ribsy* by Beverly Cleary and *Key to the Treasure* by Peggy Parish at least 30 times each.

Last week, in my basement, I found those two novels and a dozen other childhood books. Holding *Key to the Treasure* in my hands again brought back memories of my Arkansas grandparents so I carried the book upstairs and reread it.

My maternal grandparents were Kansans, born and raised. However, before I came into this world, they moved from Larned to a place in the country southwest of Fayetteville, Arkansas. Once or twice a year, my family made an eight-hour drive to their house in the Ozarks.

For the final leg of the journey to their home, we left a paved road and drove past Dowell Cemetery, a shady rural graveyard filled with moss and old gray stones. A few miles later we arrived at their house, hidden from view of the road by a thick row of spirea bushes.

Grandpa built the small, simple house in 1952. They lived there until I was about 7, so all I have are little-girl memories of the place.

Even though I was young, I clearly remember the colors of Fiestaware bowls into which my grandmother spooned sliced cling peaches. Whenever I come across that exact shade of dusty rose or soft yellow, I think of Grandma's dishes.

The well on their property had gone dry so they hauled in water. Because water was a luxury, the outhouse was used. I ran to Grandpa one day when I found a snake on the outhouse floor. Spiders and webs were creepy also, but in a less dramatic way.

Behind the house, Grandma kept an ever-expanding flower

garden. She pointed out new plantings, mostly wildflowers that she and Grandpa had dug up from the Arkansas ditches.

Further back in the yard, in a grove of hickory trees, brown and white bunnies lived in rabbit hutches.

These images remain vivid today, probably due to my repeated reading of *Key to the Treasure*.

The book was published in 1966, which was about the time my grandparents left the farm.

*Key to the Treasure* tells about three siblings who spend summers in the country with their grandparents. The kids investigate places on the property while trying to solve a family treasure hunt that dated back to Civil War days.

Naturally, as a young reader, my mind set *Key to the Treasure* at my grandparents' house in the country. Even though the Fayetteville place didn't have a stream, my imagination could easily add one behind the rabbit hutches.

When the kids in the book sat down to meals, in my mind they were eating off the Fiestaware that my grandmother had. When those kids washed supper dishes, they were standing at my grandmother's sink.

Over the past several decades, while reading all kinds of books, I've often resurrected the Fayetteville property and placed many characters in my grandparents' home. When a novel includes a scene with a well-tended garden, my imagination defaults to Grandma's patch of wildflowers.

If a poem mentions owls, I'll recall sleeping in Grandma and Grandpa's front bedroom. With windows wide open on summer nights, I heard the Arkansas owls hoot. And when a short story tells about a character that killed a snake, a photograph taken at my grandparents' home comes to mind — Dad is standing near the house with a hoe in one hand, and from his other outstretched arm dangles a long, dead snake.

Familiar childhood locations serve us time after time; they resurface when we read.

My grandparents' property is the setting for dozens of stories — some that actually happened there and many that didn't.

*May 2011*

# TANKS

In April, I took a few days off to visit my mother who lives near Hot Springs, Arkansas. On my way, driving through Fayetteville, I noticed a sign pointing to Prairie Grove Battlefield State Park.

Without a second thought, I veered onto the exit ramp. It was certainly worth a visit again after all of these years.

I was excited, because once I saw the Prairie Grove sign, I hatched a plan. When I got to the battlefield, I would photograph one of the park's World War II army tanks (or an M40 carriage gun, whatever the case may be) and send it via cell phone to my brother in Alaska along with the text "Tanks!"

In my plan, Leon then would reply with the appropriate response: "You're welcome." And, since he was likely aware that I was in Arkansas, he would immediately realize that I was at Prairie Grove, a place we both enjoyed visiting as children.

Along the eight-mile route to Prairie Grove, I drove through Farmington, a small town which holds additional memories for me. Grandpa's brother, Fred, and Fred's wife, Gladys, lived here in the '60s.

My maternal grandparents and three of my grandfather's siblings, although they had all been born and bred in Kansas, had, before I was born, moved to the Fayetteville area.

On childhood visits to Arkansas, my nuclear family along with my grandparents would make regular stops in Farmington to see Fred and Gladys.

In the '60s, their ranch-style home had a well-ordered living room where we would sit for the family conversation. We'd all catch up on who was where and who was doing what. I'd hear about their adult sons — Fred, Bob and Dick — whom I knew only from the framed photographs on the living room shelves.

Leon and I sat quietly and I'm sure restlessly, waiting for the conversation to fade into "It was nice to see you again."

Although my family had always been one to drive around and look at scenery, as a kid I became bored on those Arkansas day trips. While the adults were sufficiently amused by looking at trees and wildflowers, I wanted to get out and do something. Intrigued by the colorful billboards, I would have welcomed a stop at Dogpatch, an amusement park with a Li'l Abner theme.

We did get a chance to play at Prairie Grove Battlefield and it was probably after those visits in Farmington that we stopped at the park. There, Leon and I were able to run and shout and climb on the army tanks, which, to the imagination of a 4-year-old seemed more like pirate ships than war machines.

We have family photos of Leon and me, as little kids, neither of us much bigger than a haiku, standing in front of these massive military sculptures. And those tanks got us started on an endless series of "tanks/you're welcome" jokes, of which we never tired.

Historically speaking, Prairie Grove is a Civil War battlefield. On December 7, 1862, about 2,700 soldiers were killed or injured here. And, at some point during the past 40 years, the scene has been returned to a more Civil War–appropriate setting.

In other words, on this recent visit, I couldn't find the World War II tanks. I was very disappointed that I couldn't see them, or touch those tangible childhood memories, or send a photo of them to my brother.

Perhaps we romance certain things in our minds, turn them into something more than they were. I remember the tanks with such fondness, and I'm sure that's because it was a happy family time, an opportunity for outdoor play with my brother, and the beginning of a running family joke.

I guess all I can say at this point is "Tanks for the memories."

*January 2013*

# WHAT REMAINS

When I noticed the downhill-sloping sidewalk in front of my grandparents' former house, I remembered being 8 years old, holding onto Grandpa's hand, and skipping beside him on the way to the neighborhood grocery store.

We each have latent memories, things that we forget about until we return to the scene of that memory. In this particular case, the scene was Siloam Springs, Arkansas.

In November, Dave and I met my mom in northwest Arkansas and we drove around the area, visiting spots familiar to Mom and me. My grandparents had been native Kansans, but during my childhood they lived in Arkansas.

After nearly four decades away, I expected that my grandparents' old house might be in disrepair, but it was in fine shape and even still painted blue-gray.

While we were at this house in Siloam Springs, although we were only on the outside of it, I felt the presence of my grandparents so much here. And I wondered, how much of yourself stays behind when you leave a house? Not only did it feel as if my grandparents' spirits were here, it seemed as if they were nudging me toward memories.

Memory is something of a correspondence course. What we remember from childhood is far away from us in time and often in place. Until we get that time machine fixed, we can't return to a particular time, but sometimes, if we're lucky, we can revisit places we once knew well.

It was thrilling to suddenly recall that scene of walking with Grandpa that block-and-a-half to the store for milk or potatoes. A new/old memory.

An ongoing sadness in my life is that I didn't get to experience my maternal grandparents during my adult years. Grandpa died when I was 16 and Grandma passed away when I was 18.

I'm always searching, it seems, for these people who loved me, for the grandfather who laughed at my antics, who scooped me up and carried me around. I'm still looking for my grandmother who sewed dresses for me and sent handwritten letters.

Driving around, I was surprised that so much of what I remembered from those trips to Arkansas in the '60s and '70s was still there, the grid of my childhood still intact.

It was fun to be able to show these places to Dave. And I felt fortunate to be able to visit them with my mom. With Mom beside me it felt like a treasure hunt, trying to find what was left of those long-ago settings.

Of the three places my grandparents had lived when I was growing up, this two-story house in Siloam Springs was my favorite. It was a spacious house, and with four bedrooms upstairs I had my own room when we visited.

When I caught sight of the small part of the house that jutted out on the south side, I remembered sitting on an oval rug in that room to watch Art Fleming on *Jeopardy* on an ancient (even then) black-and-white television set.

My uncle and aunt and four cousins lived just up the alley from this house. In my grandparents' backyard in the evenings, the adults would sit in lawn chairs and talk while we kids turned cartwheels in the grass until the moon and stars lit the night.

When we return to a place of our youth, we look for what remains.

Memories somersaulted through my mind. Seeing that house again was a joy. Although my grandparents departed years ago, in a way they were still there.

*Navigating Our Lives*

*April 2010*

# THE ROADS TAKEN

It was the dark side of dusk when I left Amy's house in Lenexa.

As I backed out of my friend's driveway, I punched "Go home" on the screen of my GPS, counting on that British voice I call Daniel to deliver me home, one hundred miles away.

Having a GPS has made me much more willing to visit Kansas City on my own. All I need is an address and the dutiful Daniel will take my hand and lead me there. If I miss a turn, he's as quick to correct me as my ruler-wielding sixth-grade teacher.

After wandering around in the city, no matter how lost I get on that cluster of concrete, when it's time to go home, my electronic buddy can put me southbound on Interstate Highway 35.

Although I'm not really comfortable driving the freeways in a large city, what with all the merging and lane-changing going on at reckless speeds, I do like to drive.

Actually, I love to drive, always have, ever since I received my first driver's license and signed my name on it with the optimistic handwriting of a teenager. Back then, those paper driver's licenses had no photos (so, actually, yes, those were the good old days).

As a teenager, I never drove far — and I still seldom get more than 150 miles from home, but I do like to wander. Driving is pure freedom; every intersection is an option and all options are on the table.

As I drove home from Kansas City that evening, I sifted through the day's events in my head. I had gone to Lenexa to have dinner with Amy in honor of her 50th birthday. I'm a year ahead of her; today is number 51 for me, and except for a broken bone in my foot, year 5-0 turned out exceptionally well. It's definitely a year worth celebrating and I wanted to pass that on.

Before the trip, I had told my brother that I was going to visit Amy for her birthday. Because she and I had been inseparable during our youth, Leon knew good and well how old she'd be, but he responded, "Amy is 50? That can't be. Please check your math."

When you hit 50, that large of a number does seem hard to account for, because not all that long ago, Amy and I were barefoot little girls avoiding stickers on the sidewalks between our homes. If I could still feel the soft coating of Pawnee Rock dust on my feet, how could we possibly be this old?

Back on the interstate, I enjoyed the drive home. The blackness detached me from the landscape, from the real world, and that put me alone with my thoughts in the peaceful tunnel of night. I came upon a rolling gang of gasoline tankers. Sandwiched between them was not a place I cared to be, so I passed all four.

I replayed the conversation Amy and I had just had on her backyard deck where we had dined on Chinese take-out on a glorious evening, surrounded by all the color and warmth of April.

Amy and I talked about decisions we had made: college, relationships, career options, right turns, wrong turns, how we had each ended up where we are. At 18, neither of us had any real idea about our future; we had each simply picked a direction and headed off blindly. A GPS that offered informed career choices sure would've been helpful back then.

But perhaps the roads we took were the right ones. Maybe life simply comes down to driving in the dark, staying out of the way of gasoline trucks, keeping one's options open, and celebrating birthdays with dear friends.

*December 2012*

# LOOKING FOR JOY

It was the third week of December 1986. Depressed, I sat alone in my new apartment.

The divorce from my first husband had been finalized that week. I had always been pretty good at solitude, but being alone in an empty living room plunged me into the abyss.

One evening, I watched a made-for-TV movie starring Marlo Thomas called *It Happened One Christmas.*

The movie was a remake of *It's a Wonderful Life* — which I had never seen, so the movie was fresh for me. The show began with Marlo as a woman in despair. I could relate. Bleeding from the wounds of grief, I wasn't exactly exuding holiday joy myself.

Like every Christmas show, this movie was designed to open one's heart. And the movie did its job; it pulled me out of the darkness, cauterized my wounds, offered me solid ground on which to walk. For the first time in months, I felt happy.

That movie changed me. And so that's why, decades later, every December, even though I would certainly never admit it to anyone, I watch Christmas movies. I watch every cheesy, overly sentimental and Scrooge-inspired movie that I can.

The stories may be about a boy who buys red dancing shoes for his dying mother, a corporate employee too busy for Christmas or a child teaching a harried parent the true meaning of the holiday. What's in it for me? I want to see the softening of hearts. I want to see people doing good things for others.

Recently, I ran across an obituary I clipped from *The Emporia Gazette* in January of 2009 for Billy Cook, who died at age 75. The obit listed no occupation but said that Billy had been born in Nebraska and graduated from Emporia High.

I didn't know Billy Cook personally, and yet I saved his obituary. I had wanted to remember him because there was something about Billy that inspired me.

When I moved to Emporia in the '80s, Billy was a fixture downtown. Daily, he walked along Commercial Street and picked up trash. Billy had a constant grin and said hello to people he encountered.

Billy Cook was a one-man clean-up crew for downtown Emporia. I don't know what his motivation was, but it doesn't really matter, does it? He performed a service, keeping our downtown litter-free, and he did it with a light spirit and seemingly with joy.

His obituary wasn't lengthy. Billy had one survivor, a sister in Overland Park. What touched me in the clipping from the Gazette was one particular line: "Mr. Cook was best known for the many things he did for the betterment of Emporia."

It was a quiet little line that said so much.

We don't have to do big things to make a difference in the world. Sometimes what matters most is simply to do whatever job or duty is placed before us, and to do that job with enthusiasm or delight.

In our messy lives, what we're all really looking for, I think, is peace and joy. So we reach for inspiration wherever we can find it — in sappy Christmas movies, or maybe in the memory of a man who once picked up litter from the city's streets.

When we see people do good deeds, we are inspired to contribute our own style of goodness to the world. And when we ourselves do kind things, that's when the joy sneaks in.

*December 2010*

# CHRISTMAS EVE

When I was a kid, the thought of an onstage appearance terrified me. When I was 5 years old, preparing for my first Christmas Eve performance, I practiced my line 17 million times. I played those four words over and over until they left a permanent crease in my brain.

Every year at the Pawnee Rock Bergthal Mennonite Church, each Sunday school class presented a Christmas Eve poem or a skit. And the congregation rounded out the evening with Christmas carols.

My class was to recite a poem about the stars over Bethlehem and each of us had one line to deliver. Dressed in white choir robes, we each carried a star-on-a-stick, the cardboard stars cut from cereal boxes and covered with aluminum foil.

I didn't want to flub my line. My parents were in the audience, my brother, my friends, grandparents and Grandma's sisters, Ella and Clara. Well, actually, I was related to nearly everyone in the congregation in one way or another.

Our ancestors came over on the same boat. Literally. In 1874, after sailing to America on the steamship *City of London*, about 30 Mennonite families found their way to the Pawnee Rock area in Barton County.

Their passports had been delayed for months so rather than arriving in Kansas in early spring, they got here in November. Because they had no time to build shelter before the snow hit, the Santa Fe Railroad provided boxcars for housing that first winter.

Over the decades, the congregation built several churches. The brick building currently in use was constructed in 1915 about three miles north of Pawnee Rock. It's on a rise, surrounded by pastures and farmland.

On a winter's evening, stepping inside the church felt like a warm embrace and the background murmur of voices was low and comforting.

The sanctuary was always packed for the Christmas Eve program. Kids came home from college. Families returned from Chicago or Dallas or from wherever their jobs had flung them.

And on that evening when I was 5, my classmates and I walked onto the stage. Our teacher lowered the microphone and nodded at me. I stepped up, the star-on-a-stick clutched in my sweaty grip, and I recited my line without flaw: "I am a star."

In the years since I moved away from home, I've returned maybe a half-dozen times for the Christmas Eve program. As an adult, you watch the children perform and you find yourself leaning in, willing them to do well, so that they'll feel proud of themselves.

It's been quite a few years since I attended the church's Christmas Eve program, but a sideline scene from one particular night has stayed with me.

In my line of vision, I could see Shelly Boele-LeRoy, who was holding her infant, Andrew. The baby was in Shelly's lap, facing her, and in the middle of the evening's program Andrew spit up on her, making a huge mess.

I watched this mother as she found a fresh cloth and cleaned first her infant and then her own black dress, and she did this without drawing attention, without a wrinkle to her nose, without a single look of disgust. I was taken by Shelly's serenity, her calm countenance, the tenderness in her touch.

"O Holy Night" and "Joy to the World" were among the hymns sung that evening, but the song I carried home with me was "Silent Night." One moment of a mother's unconditional love made real the scene of "'round yon virgin, mother and child." And what I observed was nothing less than "love's pure light."

*June 2009*

# PLANE GEOMETRY

Kansas stands out on the U.S. map.

When TV meteorologists forecast the national weather, our eyes are drawn to the state that is smack dab in the center of the screen.

But to some coastal folks, especially those who will never wander into the middle of the country, Kansas is indistinguishable; it's merely "one of those rectangular states."

Believe it or not, some people can't tell Kansas from Nebraska.

Like those sibling states above us, Nebraska, North and South Dakota, Kansas has a basic rectangular shape. And, like our northern neighbors, we don't mind living in a boxy world.

When the puzzle pieces fall out of the map, it's easy to recognize Kansas: three square corners and one minor mishap — the Missouri River cuts a squiggly chunk out of our northeast corner and awards it to the state of Missouri.

Before statehood, we didn't have the same shape. In the 1850s, the Kansas Territory came equipped with a panhandle. Back then, Kansas stretched beyond Denver. That city was named for James Denver, who served as Kansas Territorial Governor in 1858.

If we had kept that chunk of western real estate, Mount Sunflower (elevation 4,039 feet) would not be Kansas' highest point.

With the exception of some rolling hills and a few odd-shaped rock formations, Kansas was a smooth plane of endless grass.

Kansas must have looked like a huge sheet cake to the European settlers who couldn't wait to cut it into little square pieces. As the Santa Fe Railroad was built, the land was divided among homesteaders.

Using the horizon as a template, the lines of Kansas were drawn. Most of our 105 counties are in the shape of parallelograms. Inside of those counties are townships and most of those townships are square or rectangular as well.

The Kansas map is full of right angles and straight lines. As you drive west, the lines (and roads) become straighter and the squares become more obvious.

Kansas has more right angles than a geometry book. So if you're fond of rectangles and squares and straight lines, this is a happy place to be.

In the western half of the state, a curve in the road is an event. My cousin Dave Crabtree, who used to be an over-the-road truck driver, once remarked, "Kansas is a dream to drive in; you don't even have to aim."

U.S. Highway 56 roughly follows the old Santa Fe Trail, and the section of U.S. 56 that passes through my hometown of Pawnee Rock is on a diagonal. But most roads in Kansas are of the east-west or north-south variety. And so in order to travel in a southeasterly direction, one would need to turn left, then right, left, then right, similar to the jagged moves a child makes on an Etch-A-Sketch.

I was raised with the grid and its dependable mile roads. In central Kansas, if you are given directions to travel five miles north, there's no need to watch the odometer, you just count crossroads. Intersections show up, as expected, at each and every mile.

The layout of Kansas gives us a solid base to work from. It provides an underlying structure to our lives. If the events of the world seem a little chaotic, we can drive through the flat land of Kansas and take comfort in its predictable order.

It's all geometry, plane and simple.

*June 2011*

# AS WE WANDER

One of the joys of Kansas is that the scenery is simple and uncluttered — and that also makes it easy to focus on one thing at a time.

But because our minds like to chew on something, the brain employs the eyes to scan the horizon and find something to contemplate. We like to solve riddles, fill in the blanks; we want to know the rest of the story.

Maybe we'll see a patch of yellow irises where they seem out of place, blooming along a rusty barbed-wire fence. So then we look for a driveway nearby or some evidence that the land was once a farmstead, because irises don't just pop up out of nowhere.

Down the road our eyes may settle on a falling-down outbuilding and wonder how long it will lean before the nails just let go. Then we may think about the lumber becoming one with the earth, and roly-polys curling under the rotting wood, half-buried in the cool, damp dirt.

An abandoned barn holds onto its nobility like a weathered gray castle, even though the paint has been worn off by wind and rain and the windows and doors have become black holes of mystery.

When I was a kid riding in the car, I stared out the window and whatever we drove past, I tried to figure out how that thing worked. I was curious about how a pivot irrigation system walked its way around the fields, and what the oil well "horses" did with the oil they were supposedly pumping, or why Aermotor in Chicago couldn't make a metal windmill that didn't shriek in the breeze.

And, as a youngster sitting in the backseat of the car, one day I noticed that some of the telephone poles along the highway were taller than others. There would be a long stretch of regular-height poles, then taller ones, then regular-sized poles again.

I didn't ask my mom for the answer, I just studied the rhythm of the poles and finally realized that the taller ones were placed on either side of the mile roads, to allow for high-clearance vehicles to pass underneath.

Although I have only a casual acquaintance with cattle, the manner in which they place themselves in a field has always fascinated me. Cattle are cocktail-party animals. They're social; they hang out together.

With cattle, I always check to see if they're facing the same direction. That habit I blame on Mark Twain. Ever since my grade school days, I've been carrying in my mind a scene from *The Adventures of Huckleberry Finn.*

In the story, Huck puts on a dress and a bonnet and goes to town to learn whether or not the community fell for his staged murder. Pretending to be a girl, Huck stops at a house and visits with a woman. Curious about his odd behavior, the woman questions him.

One thing she asked was, "If fifteen cows is browsing on a hill, how many of them eats with their heads pointed in the same direction?" Huck replies, "The whole fifteen, mum."

"Well, I reckon you have lived in the country. I thought maybe you was trying to hocus me again."

Heaven only knows why that one particular scene in the story stuck with me, but it's been riding along in my brain like a fact-checker for years. And I keep trying to prove it. Sure, in real life, most cattle in a field are facing the same direction while eating, but there are always one or two rebel cows aimed a different way.

So that's how I've spent my adult life, trying to mentally will cattle to all face the same direction. I want to make Huck Finn right.

This state may have a quiet landscape, but there are certainly enough things out there to occupy one's mind along the Kansas roadways. We can always find something to wonder about as we wander about.

*January 2011*

# THEY CAME TO STAY

As last week's winter storm began to move across the state, my mind returned to a trip I took to northwest Kansas in October.

Traveling I-70, it was around Russell that I began to notice the hinged barricades at the entrance ramps, gates used to close the highway during blizzards.

The gates caught my eye because we don't have them on the interstates in eastern Kansas. Their existence says, "We've had blizzards here before. We expect more."

When I think of pioneers, my mind tends to land in the northwest region of Kansas. The ones who settled there must have been incredibly tough people. Winter hits northwest Kansas first. And it hits there hardest.

"There is no doubt that once you get west of the 100th meridian, blizzards become much more severe, the wind becomes higher and there are fewer trees and hills to slow the wind," Mark Bogner, meteorologist with KSN-TV in Wichita, told me via e-mail.

Bogner mentioned a couple of previous storms at Goodland, the kind of blizzards that likely also struck when pioneers lived in sod houses, rustic homes or even dugouts. A November 1983 blizzard "produced 21.7 inches of snow with a peak wind gust of 49 mph," Bogner said. Another, in November, 1975, "had 13.2 inches of snow with a peak wind gust of 68 mph!"

Colby, which calls itself "The Oasis on the Plains," pays tribute to its pioneer heritage in various ways. In front of the Thomas County Courthouse is a sculpture called *Spirit of the Prairie* by Charlie Norton. The statue is of a pioneer woman gazing to the horizon, a toddler on her hip, her other arm raised high waving her bonnet.

The public library in Colby is called Pioneer Memorial Library, and near the interstate is the fabulous Prairie Museum of Art and History which shows and tells about life on the plains. There is even a sod house on the grounds, which is actually a very homey structure and seems like it would make a decent fort against the elements.

Fascinating firsthand narratives about those early settlers can be found in *Pioneer Women: Voices from the Kansas Frontier* by Joanna L. Stratton. It's a collection of writings by women who were among the first to set up residence in Kansas. Those stories recount not only the viciousness of winter on the plains, but also other forms of danger, such as Indians, prairie fires, the difficulties of plowing virgin soil, droughts, rattlesnakes, grasshoppers, wolves, isolation and exhausting winds.

The early days on the Kansas prairies were certainly challenging, but many survived those tests of will and strength.

In the book, Stratton quotes an unidentified writer, "'It may seem a cheerless life,' mused one woman, 'but there were many compensations: the thrill of conquering a new country; the wonderful atmosphere; the attraction of the prairie, which simply gets into your blood and makes you dissatisfied away from it; the low-lying hills and the unobstructed view of the horizon; and the fleecy clouds driven by the never failing winds. The pioneer spirit was continuous in our family.'"

In the 1800s, many settlers began new lives on the High Plains. They didn't find Kansas an easy row to hoe. Some fled, of course, and returned to the East. But many made it their home. Kansans, by nature, seem to be independent and resourceful, and in the sparsely populated northwest region, they have to be.

During that October trip, Goodland was also one of my stops. On the Sherman County Courthouse lawn is a life-size sculpture by Greg Todd.

The bronze piece portrays a man and a woman standing next to a plow. And for me, the four simple words of the sculpture's title sums up the lives of those hardy pioneers: *They Came to Stay.*

*February 2012*

# THE ALLEY

A small town is pieced together with alleys.

As a teenager, I ran through shadow-filled alleys after dark, playing hide-and-seek with classmates. I hung on in the backseat as a friend fish-tailed her Suburban through snowy alleyways at night. And sometimes I rode my bike down the alleys, its tires slowed by the thick sand.

Recently, while looking at photographs of Pawnee Rock, I paused when I saw a picture of our family alley.

It wasn't actually our alley; it was in the block to the south of us, but I think our family used it more than anyone else. It was one of the pathways my mom, dad, brother and I walked to get downtown, to where my mom worked — the post office and the dress shop, to my dad's woodworking shop, to the grocery store.

When I was young, skipping alongside Mom or Dad, I might have chased a butterfly or stopped at a patch of clover to look for four leaves. The paths of our childhood may be where our poems begin.

We can all think of various pathways in our lives. Maybe we recall our walking route to grade school or to English 312. Perhaps you're thinking of the worn line in the grass between the parking lot and your office. Along these trails, these sidewalks, these alleyways, we've carried our thoughts, our sorrow, our joys.

My favorite thing about this particular alley was that it was adjacent to what I called "the forest." In Kansas, if you hold your arms straight out, spin in a circle, and hit two or more trees with your hands, that's a forest.

I think this lot was originally a tree nursery before I was born, but in my time it was a fairly dense, tree-filled place with shaggy underbrush and even a caved-in cellar. One had to climb over a lazy fence to get in, but the forest was a good hideout for a kid, especially one who watched *Daniel Boone* and liked to pretend she was an Indian.

The other day, when I came across the photograph of that alley, I thought about how there is more meaning to this alley than is visible in a picture.

In that photo, there are things that only I can see. I recalled the day I turned 8. I galloped down that alley to get the mail and felt like the luckiest kid on the planet. My mom had just told me that I had a new cousin, Doug, and that he had been born on my birthday.

I remembered one day, walking home from the Pawnee Rock Dress Shop, where I had purchased, for a dollar, a pair of tiny folding scissors in a red vinyl pouch to give to my mom for Mother's Day. I thought about how excited she would be to have this tiny pair of scissors.

Occasionally, Mom put 61 cents into my palm and sent me on a mission. At Carris's Grocery Store, I'd walk through the screen door and across the wooden floor to order a pound of hamburger. At the meat counter, Mr. Carris scooped ground beef into a paper tray, weighed it, wrapped it, and wrote 59 cents on the butcher paper. In the front of the store, Mrs. Carris collected the 61 cents and I'd walk home with the main ingredient for supper.

That alley took me to the post office thousands of times to collect mail from Box 7. When I got letters from my Arkansas grandma or from a pen pal, I'd open the envelopes right there and read the letters while walking home.

We've each left our footsteps and our thoughts on various pathways in our lives. And we can go back anytime to retrieve those memories; they're still there, right where we left them.

*August 2012*

# A RETURN TO MAYBERRY

While I was growing up in the '60s, I noticed that my grand-mother seemed to prefer the days of her youth over the current times.

Grandma clung to the old ways. On wash day, she used her wringer washer on the porch. At bath time, she heated water on her stove and carried it to the bathtub rather than use the new-fangled water heater. When nature called, Grandma visited the wooden outhouse tucked away in the shelterbelt.

She spoke longingly about the good old days, which to us grandkids didn't sound that good at all. We liked indoor plumb-ing, electricity, television and telephones.

Maybe Grandma clung to the past because the '60s were a time of big changes and dramatic events: the assassinations of John and Robert Kennedy and Martin Luther King Jr., the Viet-nam War and the protests, the civil rights movement, the nuclear threat from Russia.

It was a scary world then and Grandma found comfort in the old ways.

It's a scary world now, and I find comfort in the black-and-white reruns of *The Andy Griffith Show*. When Andy died in July, I think we all returned to Mayberry in our minds.

The show aired from 1960 to 1968. Even after 50 years, the show holds up. Mayberry is symbolic of what we long for in society — a place where people get along, where folks work to-gether toward a common goal.

Mayberry represents a place of safety, and it doesn't seem too different from the hometown of my childhood. Many people in Pawnee Rock left the keys in their cars and their houses un-locked. If I didn't put my bicycle away at night, I knew it would be there in the morning. Nowadays, we lock everything. There are safety seals on ketchup bottles and we go through metal detectors at the courthouse. We live in a culture of fear.

In the fictitious world of Mayberry, a spare key to the town's drug store was kept on top of the door frame and the sheriff didn't carry a gun. However, most of the problems Andy faced weren't of a criminal nature. He dealt with quirky personalities and awkward situations, and he handled them with patience and with common sense. And always with kindness.

Andy, Barney and Opie would rather eat dozens of Aunt Bee's awful-tasting pickles than hurt her feelings.

On one show, Barney suggested that Andy run a suspicious person out of town and Andy said something like, "If I was to run everybody out of town that was actin' strange, I figure I'd empty the whole town."

Even though Barney's antics could annoy Andy, Andy never tried to fix him. He just let Barney and all the other residents be who they were. And is there not a better friend than someone who understands our idiosyncrasies and accepts us just as we are?

In an interview Andy Griffith once described the show like this, "It was about love. Barney would set himself up for a fall and Andy would be there to catch him."

My grandmother held onto the past. Often these days, I find myself wishing for the simpler times as well.

What many of us long for, I think, is what those folks had in Mayberry: the small-town pace, the sense of connection, the friendliness, the wisdom of Andy Taylor.

We may not be able to do anything about a world that seems to be spinning crazily out of control, but perhaps we can create in our own lives those things that were found in Mayberry — a strong sense of community, kindness and acceptance, love and respect for one another.

*April 2014*

# THE VIEWFINDER

Do you know what I miss? I miss having a viewfinder. I have to admit, taking photographs is easier with my phone than using a real camera. I don't have to close one eye and peer through that tiny viewfinder. And I hardly even have to aim. Point, and shoot. And later, using a handy phone app, I can crop the photo to meet my needs.

Things were much different back in the olden days when I used an actual camera, one with film.

My interest in photography began when my brother took up the hobby. As Leon's little sister and biggest fan, I wanted to do whatever he did.

One September evening in 1972, during my eighth grade year, I took our family's Brownie camera to the junior high football game. I shot some blurry far-off photos of the game, but mostly I took blurry pictures of my friends acting like their 13-year-old selves.

A few years later when my brother upgraded, I inherited his single-lens reflex camera. Leon taught me how to roll my own 35 mm black-and-white film and develop it, and how to print photographs in his darkroom.

After Leon left for college, I took his place on football sidelines and under the basketball hoop, that heavy camera hanging around my neck. And like my brother once had, I stayed up until 2 on Saturday mornings printing Friday night sports photos. I mailed them to Larned before noon on Saturday and they were published in Monday afternoon's *Tiller and Toiler* newspaper.

During my high school years, my mom and I occasionally took rides in the country. This tradition began when she taught me how to drive at age 13, but the Saturday afternoon trips continued until I graduated. We drove around Barton, Rush, Pawnee and Edwards counties.

I started taking my camera along on these car trips with Mom. Although I had been on many country rides in my life, it was on these Saturday drives, with stops to look through a viewfinder, that I began to see Kansas as beautiful, Kansas as art.

Near Hoisington, at a ghost town named Boyd, I photographed what was left of an old gas station with its glass-topped vertical pumps.

In Rush County, Post Rock country, I took pictures of limestone fence posts with barbed wire wrapped around or running through the posts. And out in the sand hills of Edwards County, I photographed a weathered barn and sunflowers.

Everything was in black-and-white, but I learned I could use a polarizing filter and pull some incredible clouds out of the sky.

I had that camera against my face for pretty much my last three years in high school. And an odd thing began to happen. Even when I wasn't holding a camera, my mind would create its own viewfinder. I'd scan the horizon, and my eyes, trained to the rectangular frame, naturally searched for the shot I would take if I had my camera.

You'd think that a tiny rectangle would be very limiting; after all, there's this whole big world around you, but you can include only one small portion of it in your photo.

As in life, however, sometimes limitation can be your best friend. If you have or do too much, life becomes full of distraction and clutter, and lacking an obvious focal point.

With a photo, you're allowed one rectangle of space at a time — but you can put whatever you choose into that frame.

It's all well and good to see the big picture, but sometimes it helps to narrow one's focus, pay attention to the light and take the best shot we can.

*April 2014*

# OUR MIDWESTERN HOME

When a national weather map shows up on TV, where do we look? At the center of the screen, of course. Mapwise, Kansas is the star of the show, sitting in the heart of the country.

There are pros and cons to every state, but landwise and locationwise, this a pretty good place to be. In the middle of the country, we have a healthy mix of the four seasons, but we don't get Texas heat or Minnesota cold.

Sure, we're landlocked, but that's not necessarily a bad thing. We can get in our cars and drive well over a thousand miles east or west, or 700 miles north or south.

Last May, I took a trip with my mom to Savannah, Ga. To get there, it took more than 24 hours in the car from Emporia. After three long days of molding bodies to fit car seats, we got our reward — walking barefoot into the Atlantic Ocean at Tybee Island Beach.

Nothing could have drained away the stress of three days on the road as well as feeling the May sunshine on our shoulders, warm waves washing our shins, the tide pulling sand out from under our feet. Every problem in the world disappeared. This was surely heaven.

A huge container ship, off in the distance, moved slowly toward the horizon. In looking across the ocean, I could actually see the earth bend away from us, and I wondered how the water stays on the planet.

Years ago, on another visit to Georgia, my stepfather took us out onto the ocean in his 22-foot sailboat. We were far enough from shore to watch shrimp boats drop their winged nets to the side and then draw them back in. Seagulls swarmed the boats, diving for food. It was all very picturesque.

So I understand part of the attraction of the ocean. Well, mostly the beach part. My lack of total enthusiasm for the sea is that once you're out there, there's nothing to see through your sunburned eyes except water and sky. I can only assume it's the same view in every direction, all the way to Portugal.

Blame it on my roots: I'm a Kansan. I like dirt, earth, solid ground. I like walking, hiking. I like cars and driving. I like long straight roads. I like the plains and the prairie.

Now, it's been a long time ago, but Dave and I once visited New York City. I loved the energy there, I really did. I hope to return someday.

There's nothing like the thrill of walking into the New York Public Library and seeing those long wooden tables with the green lamps that have been shown in dozens of movies and TV shows. Dave and I walked through Grand Central Station and the beautiful Central Park. We took a carriage ride, a subway ride and a scary cab ride.

In the Big Apple, I walked with my head leaned back. I don't really understand skyscrapers, because that's not how we build things in Kansas.

We walked in shadows of buildings, never seeing the horizon, barely seeing the sky. In New York City, it seemed as if there would be no place to be alone, not truly alone. You would always be within earshot of people or of the city's noise. I worry about residents who probably never even leave the city.

And that's why I love Kansas. Within ten minutes of home, we can be out roaming the countryside. In the Flint Hills, we step onto the land and feel the heartbeat of the planet, or maybe that's just the wind beating in our ears. But we do feel the pulse of the earth as it moves through our feet and into our souls.

Like being exposed to the elements on the ocean, we, too, are vulnerable on the open prairie. Out there, thunder rolls like stampeding cattle. Lighting, hail or a tornado could take us out without a second thought. But most of the time in the Flint Hills, we feel so protected, so comforted by that buffer of space between us and the crazy world.

We are lucky to live in this state that has plenty of breathing room, plenty of wide open spaces.

This place, this place, this place. Home.

*January 2012*

# A PART OF KANSAS

By choice or by default, we live on this ancient land, with its whispers of sharks and dinosaurs, this territory where blood was shed to claim that 34th star, this state where Pluto was, is, and always will be "our planet."

This rectangle is where we spend our nights and our days. Whether we've been here for only a few months or whether we've spent our entire lives here, Kansas is home.

It is home because this is where our stories are being lived, where the days of our lives have unfolded, one at a time, until we have grown into the person we are now.

The skies over Kansas have absorbed our stories, our conversations. And like everyone who has ever spent time here, including Native American tribes and those passing through on the Santa Fe Trail, our lives have become a part of this land for all eternity.

Our existence here has been noted. This geography holds our biography.

For many of us, Kansas is where we were first placed onto the seat of a swing, where we learned how to pump our legs so we could sail high into the blue sky.

This is where we learned to let go of those swing chains, where we leaped into the air, rolling in the grass as we landed. This is where we learned about chiggers.

Here, we've hand-written letters to pen pals, to grandmothers, to lovers. We've painted our homes, raked leaves, have ridden bicycles and horses. This is where we've changed oil, hammered nails, knitted scarves.

Some of us have learned how to water ski here, we've slept under midnight blue skies with a million stars keeping watch.

We have cast a few fishing lines. We have cast a few dreams aside. We have fallen into love, we have fallen out. Many of us have exchanged vows, raised children, barbecued, listened from a jury box. We've taken in stray puppies and kittens and turtles. We've scraped windshields, shoveled snow, jumped when lightning struck nearby.

This is the state where we've laughed until tears rolled down our cheeks, sharing embarrassing moments of childhood and high school. This is where we've made mistakes, big ones, where we've fallen to our knees in grief.

We've held hands at hospital beds, worry knotted in our throats. We've stood beneath green funeral tents, the canvas snapping in the breeze as dust was returned to dust.

Here in the Flint Hills, we've listened for trains and thunder and silence. We've heard the conversations of coyotes and the wind singing in the grass.

Just as this geography, this topography, is a part of us, we ourselves have become a part of the hills, the prairies, the plains, thoroughly and completely.

Our stories are common everyday events, connections with others. One friend has gone through surgery, chemo, radiation. Another tells about the baby chicks that he kept in boxes on his washing machine until he sent them out to the farm.

The poet Muriel Rukeyser said, "The universe is made of stories, not atoms." And it's those stories, those thousands of experiences, some we've shared, some we haven't, that all linger in one way or another.

Eventually, we will each leave this state by choice or by default, but our lives and our stories will always be a part of the wind, a part of the land, a part of Kansas.

# ACKNOWLEDGMENTS

It is you, my readers and friends, who give me a reason to write. Thank you for your e-mails, your comments, and for stopping me around town, and around the state, to share your own stories.

I am grateful to Chris Walker and the entire staff at *The Emporia Gazette* for putting my words in the paper every Tuesday for more than 11 years. Each essay in this book appeared in a somewhat different form in the newspaper. Thanks also go to J. Schafer, news director at Kansas Public Radio in Lawrence, for airing a number of these essays on the radio.

Many independent bookstores as well as museums and galleries in Kansas have been great partners in selling my first book, *Flyover People: Life on the Ground in a Rectangular State,* and to them I am most appreciative. In my hometown, Town Crier Bookstore provides incredible service to customers and Kansas authors. Thank you.

Conversations with other writers have buoyed me in ways that are immeasurable. Tracy Million Simmons has been my go-to friend for regular writing discussions and debriefings. And I've basked in the warmth of creative energy emanating from other Kansas writers, especially Kevin Rabas, Amy Sage Webb, Jay Price, Caryn Mirriam-Goldberg, Kelley Hunt, Tom Parker, Lou Ann Thomas, Wendy Devilbiss, Marcia Lawrence and Dan Markowitz. The Tallgrass Writing Workshop, held annually at Emporia State University, has been a great source of inspiration.

Thanks to good friends who have supported me along the way, including Amy Kliewer, Roger Heineken, Eleanor Browning, Janet Fish, Sonda Bruce, Grace Jones, Greg Jordan and Lisa Soller.

Many of these pieces were written at the Java Cat Coffeehouse, and I'm thankful to Angie Baker for offering a comfortable space and great drinks.

My friend Mark Bogner kindly and promptly responded to countless Kansas weather questions. Thank you, Mark, for sharing your meteorological expertise.

Marci Penner and WenDee LaPlant of the Kansas Sampler Foundation are a blessing to Kansas and to all Kansans. I have been endlessly impressed not only by their tireless and enthusiastic support of rural communities, but also by their heart-filled approach in working with others. They are my heroes.

I'm grateful to my mother, who taught me how to read and write, and has also sent e-mail comments every Tuesday after reading my column online.

There is not a thank you big enough for my editor and brother, Leon Unruh, who, with such skill and grace, turned both my first book and this one from words on a page to words in a book.

I am continually uplifted by my husband, Dave Leiker, who has encouraged my writing since the day we met. An extra thank you goes to Dave for allowing me to use a few of his incredible photographs in this book.

# ABOUT THE AUTHOR

Cheryl Unruh wrote her weekly Flyover People column for The Emporia Gazette for more than 11 years. Her first book, *Flyover People: Life on the Ground in a Rectangular State*, won the 2011 Kansas Notable Book Award. Cheryl's writing has also received awards from the Kansas Association of Broadcasters, the Kansas Press Association and the Kansas Sampler foundation.

She was raised in the small town of Pawnee Rock in central Kansas and graduated from the University of Kansas in Lawrence. She lives in Emporia with her husband, Dave Leiker.

More of Cheryl's columns and writings may be found at www.flyoverpeople.net. She can be reached at flyoverpeople@gmail.com.

Dave's Kansas photos can be seen at www.prairiedust.net.